ALL ABOUT
UNDERSEA
EXPLORATION

by RUTH BRINDZE

RANDOM HOUSE, NEW YORK

allabout
books

All About **UNDERSEA EXPLORATION**

Contents

THE AUTHOR and the publisher are grateful to all those who helped in the preparation of this book, and particularly wish to thank the following:

Vice Admiral John T. Hayward, USN, Deputy Chief of Naval Operations; Commander R. L. Bufkins, USNR, head, Magazine and Book Branch, Department of the Navy; C. M. Johnson, head, Technical Information Division, U.S. Navy Electronics Laboratory; Richard C. Vetter, executive secretary, Committee on Oceanography, National Academy of Sciences; J. Lamar Worzel, professor of geophysics and assistant director, Lamont Geological Observatory; Roger Revelle, director, and Henry W. Menard, Jr., associate professor of submarine geology, Scripps Institution of Oceanography; Otto Brendel, professor of fine arts and archeology, Columbia University; Gordon Hamilton and John Mertz, Arabian American Oil Company; Charles B. Towill and Beatrice Watson, British Petroleum; David Finnie, Socony Mobil Oil Company; S. V. Collins, Collins Construction Company; James Dugan; Jerry Greenberg; and Peter Throckmorton.

All About **UNDERSEA EXPLORATION**

The Earth's oceans occupy 14 times as much space as all the land above sea level.

Chapter 1

The World Beneath the Sea

If a man from outer space were to visit our planet, he would be most amazed by its oceans. For of all the planets, as far as anyone knows, only Earth has vast, deep seas.

They cover more than 71 per cent of the surface of our globe. But even this figure does not give a complete picture. You should also consider the depth of the seas. To reach the deepest known sea bottom, man has had to plummet almost seven miles through water as black as interstellar space. And there may be chasms or basins, still undiscovered, where the oceans are even deeper. Scientists estimate that there are 300 million cubic miles of water in the oceans.

It is only natural that from earliest times men have been curious about the world beneath the sea and have sought to explore it. Some searched for riches. Others

H. Broussard

Exploring ancient cargoes, under-sea archaeologists increase our knowledge of man's past.

Carrying his own air supply, man can study fish while moving freely among them.

Jerry Greenberg

dived to sightsee. (Alexander the Great is reported to have gone down to look at the fish.) And during ancient wars there were frogmen who developed underwater techniques for sinking enemy ships.

In former times, a diver could remain under water only as long as he could hold his breath. Even today, divers using the most modern equipment can remain submerged only for limited periods. But they can penetrate deeper into the ocean. Since the development of self-contained underwater breathing apparatus—shortened to Scuba—divers can carry an air supply in tanks strapped to their backs. Thus equipped, men can swim freely in the realm of fish. They can explore, take photographs, search for treasures in sunken ships, or chip off samples of rocks to determine whether an oil field is hidden under the sea floor.

As soon as a diver crosses the frontier between air and ocean and enters the world of water, his body is subjected to increased pressure. The higher one goes in the air, the thinner and lighter the atmosphere becomes; the deeper one penetrates into the sea, the heavier is the pressure of the water. Because the sea is not man's natural environment, entering it can be compared to flying through space. But we know more about the oceans (sometimes called "inner space") than about outer space, and we have already developed practical equipment for exploring the world of water.

Submarines and bathyscaphes are engineered to withstand tons of water pressure per square inch. Cameras, television apparatus, thermometers, and radio transmitters are made not only waterproof, but also pressureproof.

Thanks to the many remarkable devices which can be sent down without human operators, we have been able to explore the deepest parts of the oceans. By means of equipment operated from the surface, we have been

In the bathyscaphe, deep-sea explorers can descend 6 or 7 miles straight down to the very bottom of the ocean.

Underwood & Underwood

From research vessels on the surface,
scientists lower instruments to study the
undersea world.

Underwood & Underwood

able to map the towering mountain ranges and deep
canyons of the undersea world. We can even clock the
exact moment when an underwater volcano erupts.

In many respects the exploration of the undersea
world is as important as probing outer space. By drilling
through the layers of sediment and rock on the sea bottom,
we may solve such scientific mysteries as the age, origin,
and composition of our planet. Were all the continents
at one time a single land mass? The undersea world
may provide the answer.

There are also immediate practical reasons for ex-
panding our deep-sea exploration. Already, in many
parts of the world, oil and natural gas are being drawn

from wells in the sea bottom. The gas used in your home may have been piped from a well at the bottom of the Gulf of Mexico. The fuel for your car may come from a submerged oil field miles off the California coast. Scientists and offshore prospectors say that thus far we have tapped only a small fraction of the oceans' mineral wealth.

Ships of all types and of many nations are now helping to solve the riddles of the seas. Passenger, cargo, and government ships are equipped with depth-recording instruments that automatically portray profiles of the bottom as the vessels proceed from port to port. But the really intensive exploring is being done by special research ships manned by oceanographers. These scientists are skilled in the use of the intricate equipment that can take pictures in the blackness of the ocean's depths or measure the speed of underwater currents never seen by man.

Although vast stretches of the oceans have not yet been explored, the unprobed area is rapidly shrinking. Even parts of the ice-covered Arctic Ocean have been charted by nuclear-powered submarines. The mysteries of the sea are being pierced, and we are discovering more and more about the exciting world under the sea.

Chapter 2

Fathoming The Ocean's Secrets

According to the records, Captain Ferdinand Magellan was the first man who tried to measure the depth of the water in midocean. The attempt was made in the year 1521, when the explorer's fleet of three ships was drifting on the blue water of the Pacific Ocean. The ships had been sailing across the Pacific for more than two months. They had started from the western end of the passage which Captain Magellan discovered near the tip of South America. (This passage, which leads from the Atlantic to the Pacific Ocean, is now called the Strait of Magellan.)

Captain Magellan was experienced in measuring the depth of shallow water by lowering a rope with a weight attached to the end. Like other skilled navigators, the

9

explorer relied on such measurements to determine his position when he was approaching land. He assumed that the nearer the ship was to shore, the shallower the water would be. Thus, by lowering a weighted line, which sailors call "taking a sounding," the explorer could tell whether land was near.

When Captain Magellan tried to take his first deep-sea sounding, he was looking for land where he could obtain food and drinking water. His ships had been at sea so long that his men were suffering from lack of food. Some had died of malnutrition.

The measuring line Captain Magellan used was only 1200 feet long, more than enough for the soundings he ordinarily made. But in the Pacific, after the entire rope had been reeled out, the weight at the end did not touch bottom. The explorer mistakenly concluded that his ship had reached the deepest part of the ocean.

For hundreds of years after Magellan's experiment, no one used a long enough rope for a deep-sea sounding. Finally, in 1840, Sir James Clark Ross succeeded in lowering a weight to the bottom of the South Atlantic. When his standard sounding line proved too short, he lengthened it by tying on another rope. He continued to tie ropes together until their total length was nearly three miles. He found that the bottom was 14,550 feet down.

Imagine the difficulty of handling a rope of such great length. Later, wire cable—which can more easily be reeled out and in—was substituted for ordinary rope.

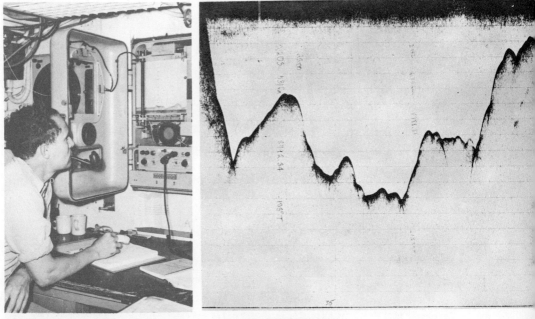

Underwood & Underwood   Lamont Geological Observatory

On an oceangoing vessel, echo-sounding equipment (left) records a depth profile of the bottom (right). See page 12.

But taking a single sounding was still a difficult and time-consuming project. It is not surprising that only a few scientific-minded navigators were willing to take the trouble of measuring the depth of the oceans.

In 1807 an ingenious scientist named Jean F. Arrago suggested a faster way for finding the depth of water. His method was to set off an explosion on the sea bottom and to time the interval before the sound was heard on the surface. Because sound travels through water at about 4800 feet per second, simple arithmetic gives the distance to the bottom.

Although echo-sounding was rarely used by seafarers, the idea intrigued inventors and they continued to develop it. About 1900 a microphone was used to detect the echo of an undersea explosion. Later, electronic equipment was developed to transmit ultrasonic high-frequency waves to the bottom and receive the return signal.

Almost all ocean-going ships are today equipped with electronic depth finders. Some show the return signal by a light on a dial divided into numbered sections, like the speedometer of an automobile. The figure to which the light points represents the depth of the water. Other more complicated echo-sounding equipment automatically makes a profile map of the sea floor. The drawing consists of a series of lines which show not only whether the underwater terrain is level or mountainous but also the location of wrecks. And when the ship is passing over a school of fish, they are shown by shadowy lines which indicate whether the fish are near the surface, midway down, or close to the bottom.

In some parts of the oceans, there is a layer of water so filled with sea life that, when first recorded by a depth finder during World War II, it was mistaken for the sea bottom. Scientists call this false bottom the *deep scattering layer*. It is located nearer the surface at night than during the daytime. No one has yet solved the scientific riddle presented by the deep scattering layer. Scientists surmise that it is composed of fish, including many shrimp-like creatures, which congregate where the most abundant food supply is to be found.

Because of the widespread use of echo-sounding equipment, details of the oceans where ships regularly travel have now been clearly defined. There still are many out-of-the-way places that have not yet been mapped, but the number of these areas is decreasing.

If all the records made by echo-sounding instruments were combined on one big contour map, it would provide a view of the undersea world similar to what might be seen if all the oceans were to dry up. A first quick glance would show that the submerged world is divided into three distinct areas—the continental shelf, the continental slope, and the ocean abyss.

Extending from all the continents is a shelf, sometimes narrow, sometimes hundreds of miles wide, which at some time may have been above sea level and part of the continental land mass. The water covering the shelves is comparatively shallow. They may be cut by canyons with steep cliffs and winding valleys. These canyons are frequently found near the mouths of rivers. For example, there is a 200-mile submarine canyon near the Hudson River and another about as big near the Congo. Some scientists believe the canyons were carved out by rivers at a time when part of the undersea terrain was above water.

At the outward boundary of the shelf, where the water averages 450 to 600 feet in depth, the land slopes suddenly downward. This is the continental slope.

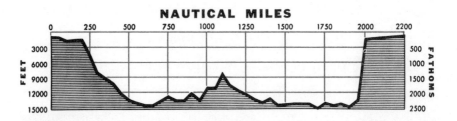

Along the route of a transatlantic telephone cable, the continental shelf appears at each end. Then the continental slope descends steeply to the abyss. In the middle rises an undersea mountain chain, the Mid-Atlantic Range.

Some of the slopes are very steep, plunging two to three miles to the abyss.

The ocean abyss, the floor of the deep sea, resembles Earth's continents. It has plains, valleys, mountains, and canyons. In the Pacific, several recently discovered ranges are notable because the mountains have peculiar flat tops. It has long been known that many ocean islands are actually the peaks of submarine mountains. Scientists surmised that the flat-topped mountains of the Pacific were once chains of islands.

Oceanographers undertook to check this theory. They dredged samples from the flat-top mountains and brought up pebbles and boulders which were as smooth and polished as rocks on an ocean beach—an almost certain sign that the flat-top mountains had once been exposed to above-water elements. Additional evidence was supplied by pieces of limestone which contained dead coral. Since coral grows only where there is sunlight, the scientists concluded that the tops of the submarine mountains had once been islands. They may have sunk as the result of changes in the earth's crust. Or they may have been submerged by the gradual deepening of the ocean as water accumulated from inside the earth. The Pacific islands started to sink, according to present estimates, about 100 million years ago, at a time when dinosaurs still roamed the continents. As far as we know, they are still sinking.

Some oceanic islands repeatedly sink and rise again. One of the most thoroughly explored of such islands is called Falcon. (The name used by people who live on nearby South Pacific islands is Fonua Fo'ou, new land.) Falcon is in an area of great volcanic activity. Three times in seventy-five years it has risen from the sea and sunk back again.

In 1952, scientists dived down to explore Falcon. They reported that in places the top was covered by

only 30 to 40 feet of water. The scenery was awe-inspiring. Black volcanic rocks rose in sharp pinnacles. Many would have been too steep to climb if the island had been above water, but the divers had no trouble swimming up and down the black cliffs. The only other sightseers were a pair of sharks and some brightly colored angel fish.

Exploring in volcanic areas is dangerous. South of Japan, the volcanic island Myojin Sho had, like Falcon, appeared and disappeared many times without injuring anyone. But in the autumn of 1952, when a Japanese research ship was floating on the sea above the island,

Underwood & Underwood

With a dredge (left), scientists obtain rock samples (right) from the ocean floor more than a mile beneath their research ship.

it erupted and blew the ship to bits. Every man aboard was killed. When another Japanese research ship arrived on the scene, the air was still clouded by steam swirling up from the undersea explosions.

Scientists in many parts of the world knew the volcano had erupted, because the sound was picked up by seismographs, instruments that have a listening range of thousands of miles. The seismographs at scientific observation points on the California coast recorded more than one hundred explosions when Myojin Sho blew up.

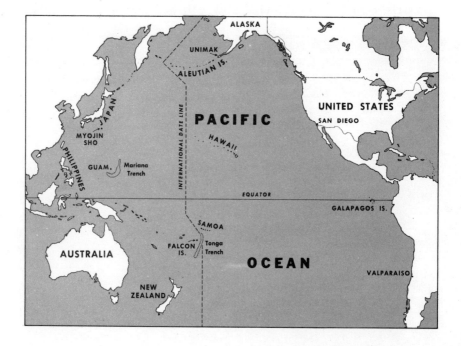

In some areas of volcanic unrest there are awesome gashes in the sea floor which scientists call "trenches." These are the deepest depressions of our planet. Falcon Island is close to the Tonga Trench, a great furrow in the sea bed which lies between New Zealand and Samoa. The Tonga Trench is 1500 miles long, 15 to 30 miles wide, and in places about 7 miles deep. If Mount Everest, the highest mountain on earth, were lowered into Tonga Trench, its peak would be covered by more than a mile of water.

Tonga Trench is being extensively explored to determine how it was formed and what creatures inhabit it. Since this trench is in an area often shattered by earthquakes, it may have been hollowed out when the sea floor split and collapsed. The resulting tidal waves probably roared over land thousands of miles away and drowned every living creature in their path.

Tidal waves or tsunamis—a name oceanographers prefer—are caused by an earthquake in the sea floor. As the bottom of the ocean cracks and buckles, water rushes into the newly formed pit and the madly swirling water gives birth to the most devastating of all sea waves. Tsunamis attain speeds of 500 miles per hour and roll on for thousands of miles.

The tsunamis that started in 1946 near Unimak, one of the Aleutian Islands, were traced with great accuracy. Seismographs at a number of Pacific coast observation stations recorded the earthquake in the sea bed near the Aleutians. The resulting tsunamis on the surface of the sea probably passed unnoticed by the navigators

In 1946, an undersea earthquake caused widespread destruction in Hawaii, 2300 miles away.

FPG

of any ships that happened to be in the area. While moving over the open sea, tsunamis are not unusually high; it is when they reach land that the waves rear up to great heights.

In less than five hours after the undersea earthquake near Unimak, the tsunamis had travelled 2300 miles and reached Hawaii. Shortly before the first great wave roared in, there was a withdrawal of water from the shore. Places ordinarily covered by deep water suddenly were exposed. It is known that water retreats as tsunamis approach. But a group of school children, unaware of the danger, went out on the beach and followed the receding water. All of them were drowned.

The tsunamis poured into valleys and toppled over houses. The onrushing water was powerful enough to lift huge blocks of concrete from their foundations and throw them on outlying reefs. The tsunamis did not stop at Hawaii but continued to roll southward. They reached Valparaiso, Chile—a distance of 8066 miles—in about 18 hours.

The Unimak undersea quake led to the establishment of a warning system. Now, as soon as an underwater earthquake is recorded, warnings are broadcast to all areas in the path of the quake waves.

The sea, like the continents, has many rivers; and those of the oceans are on a gigantic scale. The water in ocean rivers does not mingle with the water through which it passes because its temperature and salt content are different.

An amazing submarine river was discovered a few years ago in the Pacific Ocean by a young scientist named Townsend Cromwell. At the time, he was experimenting for the United States Fish and Wildlife Service with a technique called long-line fishing. The fish lines are suspended from a floating rope, several miles long, which ordinarily moves in the same direction as the waves and wind. Cromwell's rope moved in the opposite direction. This happened because the fish lines hanging from the floating rope had penetrated into a subsurface current. Strong enough to counteract the effect of the wind on the surface, it carried the entire equipment in the direction it was moving. When measurements were made of the Cromwell Current, it was found to be about 900 feet deep, 180 miles wide, and 5400 miles long. The water in the giant submarine river races through the sea in an easterly direction.

There are no turns or bends in this river; its course exactly follows the Equator. From the International

Dateline, where the undersea river starts, to the Galapagos Islands, where it suddenly ends, the Cromwell Current is centered over the Equator.

During subsequent exploration of this undersea river, the exciting discovery was made that the Equator is a real line, not just an imaginary one. The probing of the sea floor disclosed a mound along the line of the geographical Equator. This mound has been tracked in the Pacific for a distance equal to a quarter of the circumference of the globe. Further exploration may reveal that the mound follows the line of the Equator under other oceans.

Below the easterly flowing Cromwell Current, another ocean river speeds along in a westerly direction. Below this there may be others, still undiscovered.

The sediment on the bottom of the sea is the master key to the history of our world. Since the ocean basins were first filled with water billions of years ago, dead plants and animals, pieces of meteors, rocks once embedded in glaciers, and dust blown from deserts have drifted down to the bottom. In some places the sediment is miles thick, varying in color and consistency as greatly as does the earth that covers our continents.

In the North Pacific, where the ocean is of great

depth, the sediment is soft and chocolate-colored. What is the reason for this distinctive color? And why have no tiny shells been found in this ooze as they have been in other areas? To these, and to other, questions we may not have to wait much longer for answers. Oceanographers are now coring out long samples of the sea bottom. In each inch there is a clue to the early history of planet Earth.

An exciting project is being planned to bore a hole through the layers of sediment and the underlying bedrock in the hope of piercing the mysterious area usually called the Moho. This boundary zone, located below Earth's crust, is technically called the Mohorovicic Discontinuity. It was named in honor of its discoverer, Professor Andrija Mohorovicic, a Yugoslav scientist.

Wide World
Underwood & Underwood
Lamont Geological Observatory

Oceanographers prepare to lower a corer (left) to obtain samples from the ocean bottom (center). At right, deep-sea cores are stored aboard the research vessel for further study ashore.

The professor made his discovery by studying records of earthquake waves. The speed of these waves depends on the kind of rocks through which they pass. The denser the rock, the faster the waves travel through it. The professor noted two distinct high-speed quake waves. One had passed through Earth's crust. The second had traveled through an even denser formation. From the speed of the two waves and other observations, the professor concluded that below the rocks of the crust there is an abrupt change to a denser structure, the Earth's mantle. The boundary between these two layers is the Moho.

Why have scientists decided to try to pierce the Moho by drilling through the sea bottom instead of choosing a site on land? In many respects a land operation would be more convenient. But the Earth's crust is thinnest under the sea—in places only 2½ miles deep. Under the continents the average thickness of the rocky crust is 20 miles; there is no equipment for drilling such a deep hole. But scientists believe it is possible to bore through the thinner rocks of the crust under the sea. The drilling equipment will be similar to that now being used for developing undersea oil wells.

One can only guess and dream about the discoveries that will be made when a drill finally grinds into the Moho. Somewhere down there we may find a layer similar to the material on the face of the moon. By drilling under the sea we may finally learn how and when our planet was formed.

The crust of the earth.

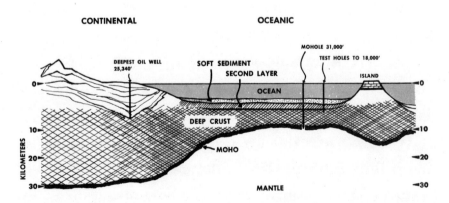

National Academy of Sciences

Chapter 3

Scientists at Sea

The Moho was discovered by clocking the speed of shock waves caused by a natural earthquake. Fortunately it is not necessary to wait for a real earthquake to gather information from shock waves. Men can make earthquakes whenever they desire by exploding charges of dynamite. Every time a depth bomb is set off, it produces an artifical earthquake from which a series of shock waves race through rocks, mud, and water. Since the speed at which the waves travel through different types of material is known, the structure of the sea bottom can be mapped, layer by layer.

The results provide a picture similar to one that might be obtained by slicing through the land under the sea. The facts obtained from shock waves indicate the thickness of each layer as well as something about the material of which it is composed.

Mapping underground formations according to the

Lamont Geological Observatory

From the shooting boat, a depth charge is tossed overboard (left). The explosion follows (right).

travel time of shock waves is called a seismic survey. Seismic comes from the Greek word *seismos,* which means earthquake. The technique of using dynamite for surveying purposes was developed by prospectors seeking underground oil wells. For oceanographers, there is no faster way of "seeing through" the sea bottom than by dropping depth bombs and timing the resulting shock waves.

Much of the preliminary exploring to find the best place to drill to the Moho was done by seismic surveying. Ordinarily two research ships operate as a team to make such a survey. It has been found that the most accurate results can be obtained by assigning one vessel —the shooting boat—to fire the depth charges, while a second—the listening boat—receives and records the quake waves.

Suppose two research ships, one of which we will call *Sea Detective* and the other *Sleuth,* are to make a seismic survey of a certain area. *Sleuth,* the shooting boat, is to fire the depth charges. *Sea Detective* is the listening or receiving boat. The plan is to map a 60-mile stretch of the sea bottom. *Sleuth* is to start dropping depth charges from a position 60 miles from where *Sea Detective* is waiting, as scientists say, "on station." The firing is to continue as *Sleuth* steams toward *Sea Detective.* The first bombs will be the standard-size Navy depth charge, containing 300 pounds of explosive. As the distance between the two boats decreases, smaller bombs will be used.

Throughout a seismic survey, the men on the firing and listening ships talk to each other by radio. Before each bomb is dropped, the man in charge of the firing announces that he is about to set off the explosion. The scientists on the listening ship indicate whether they are ready. Then the chief of the shooting team rapidly reports the data on the bomb. He tells the amount of dynamite in it and the estimated burning time of the fuse. The next announcement is a one-minute warning signal. Finally the word "Now!" comes over the radio telephone. The bomb has been fired. The exact second is noted by one of the men on the listening ship.

Before the first call from *Sleuth,* the men on the listening ship had lowered a hydrophone into the sea. This instrument contains a microphone that detects

underwater sounds. These are relayed through a connecting cable to an electronic recorder within the boat. A pen on this recording device draws a series of lines for each shock wave. Some are shown as straight lines and others as undulations. When the ships are far apart, the first wave recorded has passed through the hardest layer in the bed of the sea. The last wave has traveled through the water.

During a seismic survey, the shooting boat makes many trips back and forth across the area being mapped. During one survey in the Caribbean Sea, between Cuba and the South American coast, the shooting boat made

Lamont Geological Observatory

From the listening boat, a hydrophone is lowered into the water (left). While submerged (right), it picks up sound waves typical of undersea formations, which are recorded electrically (center).

thirty-eight runs between its starting point and the listening boat. Each time, the shooting boat turned around and, sailing a reverse course, fired another series of bombs. The data from a second series of bombs provide a check on the accuracy of the information obtained from the first. The survey in the Caribbean showed that, where the water is deepest, the sea's bedrock is thinnest.

It is most uncomfortable to ride on a shooting boat. It is also dangerous. The ship is loaded with dynamite, and handling each bomb involves hazards. As a precaution against accidents, some research expeditions limit seismic surveying to daytime hours. No seismic surveying is attempted during stormy weather.

Ships used for oceanographic research are husky but neither large nor speedy. Seaworthiness and fuel-carrying capacity are the prime requirements. Research vessels frequently travel in the most remote parts of the ocean where there are few convenient ports to replenish fuel and supplies.

Many of the ships used for exploring the oceans were originally designed for another purpose. Some were built for naval service, and others once were private yachts. When converting such ships for their new role,

additional cabins must be provided to accommodate the
scientists and space must be allotted to laboratories and
to the heavy equipment required for deep-sea exploring. The result is that the scientists and the ship's crew
live and work in cramped quarters.

All research vessels have powerful spotlights located
in strategic positions to illuminate the decks and the
ocean so that the exploring work can be continued
throughout the night. Deck space is used for storing
many of the scientists' instruments. Below deck, in the
lowest part of the ship, are huge reels wound with miles
of wire rope. Nearby is the big winch which unwinds
the miles of wire on which the heaviest instruments are
sent to the bottom.

Boxes of canned foods may be stacked near the winch.
Large quantities of food must be loaded at the beginning
of a voyage, and finding room for the food supplies is
usually a problem. Although occasionally a scientist or
crew member may catch enough fish to make a good
meal, most menus consist of food from the ship's larder.

Some oceanographic expeditions have as their object
one specific type of exploring. For example, the purpose
may be a seismic survey. Usually, however, many different types of studies are made.

The converted yacht *Saluda* (above) provides a silent sailing platform for research scientists working with the Naval Electronics Laboratory. The *Spencer F. Baird* (right), formerly a seagoing tug, has winches with wire cables up to 40,000 feet long for deep-sea research.

U.S. Navy

Underwood & Underwood

Actual samples may be dug from the sea bottom. Consider the problems involved in such an operation. First the sampling equipment must be lowered through miles of water, a procedure that takes many hours. The scientists have no sure way of knowing whether the equipment will land in a good or poor spot for taking a sample. The instrument may be caught on an outcropping of rock or strike on hardened lava. Even if the spot is a good one, the success of the probe depends on the correct functioning of many complicated mechanisms. Only after the apparatus has been hoisted up and opened do the scientists find out whether the operation has been successful. The results are frequently disappointing. But even one successful sampling operation may lead to exciting discoveries.

When the water is comparatively shallow, equipment
known as a grab may be used to collect samples from the
top layer of the sea bed. A grab has two powerful jaws
which are fixed in the open position when the equipment
is lowered to the bottom. The impact when the grab
strikes the sea floor causes the jaws to spring together.
While closing, they scoop up rocks, stones, pebbles, and
mud.

A far more complicated piece of equipment is used
to penetrate into the inner layers of the sea floor. This
valuable instrument, pictured in Chapter 2, is the corer.
It is made of hard steel tubing and is loaded with
weights. Sometimes it has a piston to force the pipe into
the sea bottom. Where the ooze and mud are thick, the
scientists may send down a corer 70 or 80 feet long.
It is often very difficult to lower a long corer and bring
it back again to the deck of the research ship. A sport
fisherman who tries to land a swordfish or a battling
tuna has a far easier time. But all the work and time
required to obtain a single long core are worth while.
Because sediment builds up slowly—sometimes less
than a quarter of an inch in a thousand years—a long
core provides clues to events in the early history of
our world. The time of an ice age can be traced by

particles of shells, and ashes provide clues to prehistoric eruptions of volcanoes.

From a study of a long cylinder of mud cored from the bed of the Atlantic, two scientists reported that about 119,000 years ago there was a rapid fall in the temperature of the sea. About 40,000 years later there was a period of temperate climate. This was followed by another ice age. The layers in the long core showed that there were alternating periods of freezing and warming until about 9000 years ago. The sea then reached about the same temperature as it has today.

It is easy to understand that digging a core from the sea bottom involves difficulties. Getting samples of sea water would appear to be a simple matter. Of course, there is no problem in securing samples from the surface. But scientists want to know about water from various depths—its chemical composition, temperature, and the vegetable and animal life the water contains. To obtain the desired samples, scientists have developed a clever device known as a Nansen bottle. (It is named for Fridtjof Nansen, Arctic explorer and oceanographer.) The metal bottle is cylinder-shaped. Both ends have caps or seals that can be closed automatically. A number of open bottles are usually strung on one wire cable.

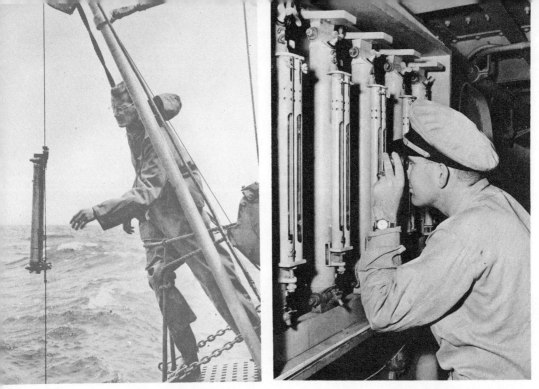

National Academy of Sciences U. S. Coast & Geodetic Survey

Nansen bottles (left) bring up deep-water samples to provide useful information about the undersea world (right).

After the string of bottles has been lowered into the sea, a weight, called a messenger, is released from the top of the cable. The messenger slides down the wire until it hits a lever attached to the uppermost bottle. At this moment a number of things happen. The lever triggers a mechanism which closes the top and bottom of the bottle, trapping the water within it. The bottle also turns over; this movement breaks the mercury column in a thermometer fastened to the outside of the bottle. The thermometer thus records the temperature of the water at the moment when the bottle was reversed. Finally the action of the lever on the first bottle releases a second messenger, which slides down the wire. When it hits the lever on the second bottle, the entire operation is repeated.

The mechanisms do not always function smoothly. Sometimes none, sometimes only a few, of the bottles are reversed. Once a water-sampling test failed because the wire cable was coated with jellyfish. The bottles had probably been lowered through a mass of jellyfish floating below the surface and the slimy tissues clogged the sampling equipment.

Fish more frequently cause trouble by biting scientific equipment. Sharks often mistake a glittering instrument for a tasty tidbit.

When oceanographers plan to lower a corer or reversing bottles, the research ship must be stopped. But scientists have many instruments that can be used while the ship is in motion. One of these is a bathythermograph, which automatically records the temperature of the water through which it is pulled. The record is made on a glass slide covered with oily smoke. The slide is so small that it can be read only with a magnifying glass.

Another instrument towed behind a ship collects

samples of plankton, the tiniest of the sea's organisms. Within the instrument are two spools of fine silk gauze. The plankton is caught on the gauze from one of the spools and is covered by gauze from the second spool. The specimens are thus automatically sandwiched between two protective layers.

Another remarkable device named a "swallow pinger" —because it was invented by Dr. John Swallow—is used to track the speed of oceanic rivers. A swallow pinger is a cylindrical tube containing a battery-operated sonar transmitter. Before the pinger is launched, weights are attached to make the instrument sink to the depth which the scientists wish to test. As the instrument is carried by the current, its transmitter sends out a steady series of signals. Picked up by receivers on the research ship, the signals enable the scientists to compute the speed and direction of the current in which the pinger is moving. No attempt is made to retrieve a pinger after its battery is used up and the signals cease. The instrument is left in the sea.

National Academy of Sciences

The bathythermograph, towed by a research vessel, records the temperature of the water.

Drift bottles, sealed with paraffin (left), are tossed overboard (right).

The old-fashioned system—and one still being used —for tracking the direction of surface currents is to toss sealed glass bottles into the sea. Within each of these drift bottles, as they are called, is a card requesting anyone who finds the bottle to furnish information as to where and when the bottle was picked up. Drift bottles are sometimes caught in fishermen's nets or tossed onto a beach by waves. Everyone who goes to the seashore should watch out for the scientists' drift

bottles. One lucky man found a bottle near the town of Bunbury in Western Australia. The bottle had been launched near Tasmania nearly seven years before, and may have traveled 16,000 miles around the world at an average speed of seven miles a day.

Much valuable information has been obtained from drift bottles. Like the data obtained from modern electronic equipment, it is steadily increasing man's knowledge and understanding of the oceans.

Jerry Greenberg

Chapter 4

Helmet and Scuba Diving

If the absence of breathable air were the only difference between conditions in our world and the world beneath the sea, it would be comparatively simple to explore under water. Providing a diver with an air supply is not a major problem. Air can be carried in

44

Peter Throckmorton

A Scuba-equipped
"free diver" works
with a helmet diver.

containers strapped like a knapsack on the explorer's back, or it can be pumped down to him through a hose.

But when man goes under the sea, he enters a completely different world, a world in which he does not really belong. Man cannot even see clearly under water. Things look out of focus, partly because light refraction is different in water, and partly because human eyes are not flat like the eyes of a fish.

This is one of the reasons why divers wear masks. Like eyeglasses, a mask corrects distortion. But even a masked diver must practice before he is able to judge distances accurately. Under water, things appear to be about one fourth larger and nearer than they actually are. A fish may seem close enough to grab although it is actually beyond reach.

But with experience a diver learns to gauge distance. Underwater hunters have proved this. The first few times a spear fisherman shoots his harpoon, it may go far wide of the mark; but with practice his aim becomes sure. In fact, so many fish have been harpooned that many states have adopted regulations similar to those that protect forest animals against over-hunting.

Sportsmen dive where the water is clear. But Navy divers and civilians engaged in salvage or construction

Using an object locator, a diver can find his target even in murky water.

projects are frequently required to work in muddy water. To help these men see through the murk, the Naval Electronics Laboratory has invented a small instrument called a "diver sonar" or "object locator." It transmits signals which are bounced back as an echo by any object in their path. The device serves the same purpose as a searchlight on a dark road. The diver turns the beam of the object locator in the direction he wishes to "light up" and then listens for a tone signal indicating the presence of some object.

All life began in, or at the edge of, the sea. One way man's early history is traced is by the chemicals in his blood; it contains sodium, potassium, and calcium in about the same proportions as in sea water. But many changes occurred after living creatures left the water.

Now when humans re-enter the watery world and wish to swim through it, they strap fins on their feet. These fins, or flippers, make swimming so easy that it is unnecessary to use arms and hands to increase speed. The diver has his hands free to pick up a lobster, to operate a camera, or to take from the bottom whatever interests him.

Yet even though a diver with foot fins can dart around like a fish, and carry the air he needs with him, he cannot roam with complete freedom in the undersea world. He cannot penetrate as deeply or stay as long as he may desire.

In all undersea activity, the pressure exerted by water is the limiting factor. Air also has weight, but all the miles and miles of air in the earth's atmosphere press down on us as we stand at the seashore at the rate of only 14.7 pounds per square inch. However, sea water is so heavy that merely 33 feet below the surface the pressure is increased by another 14.7 pounds or, as divers say, by "one atmosphere." At the 66-foot level the pressure is tripled, at 99 feet it is quadrupled. In the deepest valleys of the ocean, pressure is figured not by the pound but by the ton per square inch.

The pressure of the water affects everything in the sea—fish as well as man. Deep-sea fish have actually been seen to burst when hauled up to the surface. But man has devised ways of protecting himself against the pressure hazards of the underwater world.

We have learned how to cope with the "bends," the disease caused by pressure that can kill or cripple a diver. A French doctor named Paul Bert gave the first explanation of what happens in the human body when it is subjected to pressure. A Scot, Dr. J. S. Haldane, worked out a practical system for protecting divers. Whether a diver is encased in a helmet and full diving "dress" (which is waterproof), or wears an ordinary bathing suit and carries a reservoir of air on his back, he must not, after a deep dive, shoot up quickly to the surface. To do this may mean sudden death.

Dr. Bert's experiments proved that when man is under pressure, nitrogen is not exhaled but remains in solution in the blood. This is not dangerous so long as the diver remains under pressure. But if he makes a rapid ascent to the surface, the effect is similar to prying off the cap from a bottle of soda pop. Immediately after the cap is lifted, all the gas in the soda begins to bubble. When the nitrogen in the diver's body fizzes up, it can kill or cripple him.

In former days it was so common for divers to be crippled by nitrogen bubbles that divers thought of the bends as a natural hazard of their occupation. They were more afraid of it than of drowning or of attacks by sharks, conger eels, or octopuses.

After the cause of the bends had been established, the next step was to work out a system for permitting nitrogen to leave the body gradually. Dr. Haldane developed the first timetable to list the depths at which a diver must stop and how long he must wait before moving up to levels where pressure is less.

Divers who make deep dives must be patient men, because they may be obliged to remain under water for a long time after completing their jobs. When William Bollard, a helmet diver serving in the British Navy, made a record by going 535 feet down, he reached the bottom in 7½ minutes. His ascent took 3 hours and 1 minute.

Helmet divers whose air supply is pumped down

from the surface can usually work in deeper water, and stay on the bottom longer, than do Scuba divers. Underwater explorers who wear reservoirs of air on their backs ordinarily swim around in comparatively shallow water, for these are the regions where the most beautiful gardens and the most brilliant-colored fish are to be seen. However, Scuba divers do sometimes glide down to explore in deep water. Then, like helmet divers, they must ascend by slow stages. The United States Navy standard decompression table is the same for its helmet and Scuba divers.

When a diver goes deeper than 30 feet, his trip is regulated by a rigid schedule. And the deeper the frogman penetrates, the shorter is the time he is permitted to remain under water. According to a schedule recommended by the United States Navy, a Scuba diver who descends 120 feet is allowed exactly 18 minutes from the time he starts his descent until he leaves the bottom. And after making such a deep dive, he must wait 24 hours before diving again.

If for any reason a diver must surface before spending the required time under water, he is immediately rushed to a recompression chamber. Here the diver is subjected to the amount of pressure existing at the level where under ordinary conditions he would have been required to stop. When the diver is ready for his second "stop," the pressure is reduced. Finally—sometimes after many hours—it is safe for him to leave the chamber and to enter the lighter atmospheric pressure of our world.

Among the many things Scuba divers must learn is the importance of following a timetable. Instruction in scheduling dives is part of every course—and no one should undertake Scuba diving unless he has completed a thorough course under a trained instructor.

How does a Scuba diver know the depth at which he is operating or how many minutes he has been submerged? A helmet diver may have a telephone connection to the surface; he can be directed when to leave the bottom. But a Scuba diver, swimming around freely, must know the depth, the time, and the direction in which he is traveling. All this he can do with the help of a depth gauge, a watertight watch, and a compass.

There is another required item of equipment for Scuba and helmet divers: they must wear weights. If you were to jump into the water, either from a swimming float or from a boat, you would go down a certain distance and then bob up. The first men who tried to

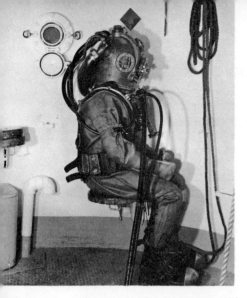

A Navy helmet diver, awkwardly weighted down, will move easily as soon as he enters the water.

stay under water discovered that the human body is buoyant. They used rocks as weights.

Modern divers use weighted belts. The ones worn by Scuba divers weigh only a few pounds, but the belts worn by helmet divers are very heavy. The 5-inch leather belt strapped around a U.S. Navy helmet diver

Captain Cousteau, with a pressure gauge on his wrist and an Aqua-Lung on his back, drives his undersea scooter.

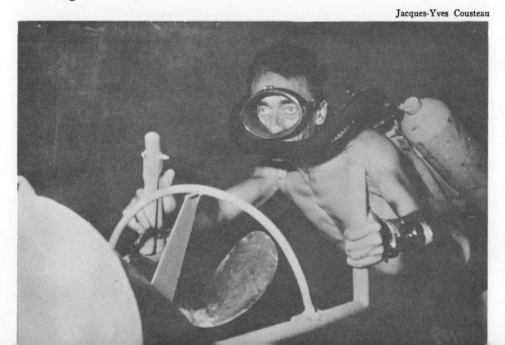

is studded with lead and weighs about 84 pounds. In addition, he wears weights on his feet. A helmet diver's boots are soled with lead plates and each boot weighs nearly 20 pounds.

When the 42-pound copper helmet is finally made fast to the diver's breast plate, which tips the scales at 22 pounds, the diver is so weighted down that it is hard for him to walk without assistance. But as soon as he enters the water, his weighted boots and the rest of his outfit no longer seem heavy.

Jacques-Yves Cousteau, the famous explorer, author, and co-inventor of the Aqua-Lung, gives the following description of the effect of water in making everything seem lighter.

"Before a camera dive, I look like a beast of burden staggering into the water with a 45-pound triple Aqua-Lung strapped on my back, four pounds of lead on my belt, and the weight of knife, pressurized watch, depth gauge, and compass on my wrists, and perhaps a 4-foot shark billy on a wrist thong. It is a relief to float my burdens in the sea and receive the seventy-pound Bathygraf cinecamera, either from two men on deck, or lowered by davit. Fully borne, myself and my gear weigh 265 pounds. Immediately under water I weigh a mere pound or so and swim head down with wonderful ease."

The scientific explanation of why things apparently lose weight when immersed in water was given more than 2000 years ago by Archimedes, a Greek mathematician and physicist. As a result of his practical experiments—some, it is said, made while he was taking a bath—Archimedes learned that water buoys up any object by a force equal to the weight of the water the object displaces.

Archimedes' principle, as it is called, is used to determine the amount of weight that must be added to overcome the "positive buoyancy" of a diver, a submarine, or anything else that is to be submerged. Suppose that a helmet diver dressed in a waterproof suit weighs 384 pounds, and that he displaces 6.5 cubic feet of water. Since one cubic foot of sea water weighs 64 pounds, the diver will displace 416 pounds of water. The difference between this figure and the diver's weight is 32 pounds —the measure of his positive buoyancy. In order to reach the bottom the diver must have "negative buoyancy." Therefore he must add more than 32 pounds to his weight.

Chapter 5

Descent by Bathysphere and Bathyscaphe

When exploring the deepest parts of the sea, man requires the protection of a rigid metal shell. A round shell is best able to withstand the tons of pressure exerted by deep water.

The first steel ball used for undersea exploring was the bathysphere. In 1934 William Beebe and Otis Barton established a record by descending 3028 feet into the sea. At this depth of a little over a half-mile, the pressure on the bathysphere was 7016 tons.

The dive was made in the Atlantic near the island of

Bermuda where the water is very clear. However, by the time the bathysphere was only 700 feet below the surface, it was so dark that when Dr. Beebe opened a book he could not tell which pages contained colored pictures and which were filled with lines of type. He reported that the illumination was "stranger than any imagination could have conceived—an indefinable translucent blue quite unlike anything I have ever seen in the upper world." As the sphere continued to go down, Dr. Beebe noted that the water appeared to be "a cold, whitish grey." Still further down he could see only "a blackish blueness."

The bathysphere was lowered from its mother ship on a single non-twisting steel cable. The sphere weighed 2½ tons. Its walls were 1½ inches thick and its interior was only 54 inches in diameter, just about enough room for two passengers and the essential equipment. Within the bathysphere were containers filled with calcium chloride to absorb moisture and with soda lime to remove carbon dioxide from the air. There was also a telephone by which the daring explorers could speak to the people on the surface ship who were responsible for reeling the wire cable on which the bathysphere hung.

The bathysphere in which Dr. Beebe descended more than a half-mile was used over a period of years by many other divers. Later, Otis Barton had another sphere built with heavier walls. This sphere was designed to withstand the pressure existing two miles down. But, like the first, it depended solely on the wire cable from which it dangled. It had to remain attached to the surface ship. The men within the sphere could not control the movement of their vehicle. And if the cable broke, the sphere would plummet to the sea bottom. There would be no way to rescue the men in the bathysphere.

What undersea explorers needed was a craft that could dive and come up by itself. The boat called the bathyscaphe can do this. The name is a combination of two Greek words, *bathy* (deep) and *scaphe* (boat). In the late 1930's, the physicist Auguste Piccard designed the first bathyscaphe. Professor Piccard had previously specialized in exploring the upper atmosphere by balloon. When he decided to descend to the depths of the sea, he designed a boat much like a blimp. The upper portion, or float, is a cigar-shaped structure which serves the same function as the gas bag of a balloon. The lower portion, or passenger gondola, is a sphere of forged steel.

The first bathyscaphe, completed in 1948, later became the property of the French Navy. After years of testing, two French naval officers dived 13,287 feet—over 2½ miles—in the bathyscaphe. This deep dive, made in 1954 near the north coast of Africa, established a new record of man's penetration into the sea. The dive was more than four times as deep as the one Dr. Beebe had made twenty years earlier.

Professor Piccard believed that a bathyscaphe could go still deeper. While engineers of the French Navy were still testing the first deep-sea boat, Professor Piccard began the construction of a second bathyscaphe. Named the *Trieste,* it was operated for several years in the Mediterranean Sea and then was purchased by the United States. It was delivered to the U.S. Navy's Electronics Laboratory at San Diego, California, in 1958. By 1960 the bathyscaphe was ready for the deepest dive ever attempted by man. The *Trieste* was scheduled to go to the floor of the Marianas Trench. This trench in the bottom of the Pacific, located about 250 miles from the island of Guam, is thought to be the deepest of all oceanic chasms.

When Lieutenant Don Walsh, the officer in charge, and his shipmate, Professor Piccard's son Jacques,

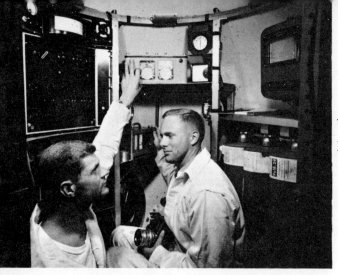

In the gondola of the *Trieste*, Lieutenant Walsh (right) and a scientist are surrounded by their instruments.

boarded the *Trieste* on the morning of January 23, 1960, they found that the bathyscaphe had suffered some damage while being towed to the site selected for the dive. Telephone wires had been ripped off, and one of the meters for measuring the rate of descent and ascent had been wrecked. The boat had another telephone system which Lieutenant Walsh could use after the bathyscaphe had submerged. But during the critical moments before starting the dive, he would not be able to communicate with the men outside while they made the last safety checks of the bathyscaphe. However, there appeared to be no damage that would affect the depthworthiness of the *Trieste*.

First Don Walsh, then Jacques Piccard squeezed through the tube leading into the steel gondola. Its inside dimensions are less than 6½ feet in diameter, and the walls are 4¾ to 7 inches thick. The apparatus for supplying oxygen and absorbing carbon dioxide is designed to maintain breathable air within the passenger chamber for 48 hours. The windows of the gondola are of clear plastic, about 5½ inches thick.

The cigar-shaped float of the bathyscaphe has thirteen tanks. Eleven of the tanks are filled with 30,000 gallons of aviation gasoline, which is lighter than water and therefore makes the bathyscaphe buoyant. One tank at each end of the float is left empty until just before the *Trieste* is to dive. Then the valves of these tanks are opened and, as sea water flows in, the bathyscaphe begins to sink. During the descent the gasoline is compressed and the empty space in the gas tanks is also filled with sea water. This is clever engineering because, in addition to serving as ballast, the water keeps the pressure inside the float equal to the pressure outside and prevents the float from collapsing.

As additional ballast the *Trieste* carries from 10 to 13 tons of small iron pellets about the size of BB shot. By releasing some of these pellets, the men within the gondola can lighten their boat and slow its descent. During an ascent, the pellets are dumped at a rapid rate.

The *Trieste* submerged at 8:20 A.M. It dived rapidly for 300 feet. There it reached the first thermocline, a

With gasoline, sea water, and tons of iron pellets, deep-sea explorers control the descent and ascent of the bathyscaphe.

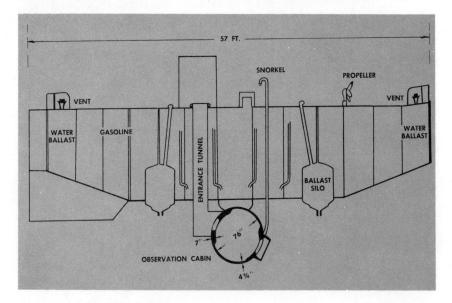

layer where the water temperature drops sharply. Since cold water is denser than warmer water, it increased the buoyancy of the bathyscaphe. To make the boat heavier so that it would continue to go down, the men released gasoline from the float.

All went well until the *Trieste* neared the 30,000-foot level. Then there was a great crack that rocked the gondola. Don Walsh later said that it felt like an earthquake. After the alarming vibration, the two men switched off their electrical instruments and waited. But there were no more quakes. When the instruments were switched on again, they indicated normal conditions. The men agreed to continue the dive.

The bottom, they thought, was only about half a mile farther down. According to the measurements made by surface probing, the depth of the Marianas Trench was believed to be 33,600 feet. But when the *Trieste's* depth gauge indicated that level there was no sign of the bottom. Since the hydronauts did not know how far they were above the sea floor, the men released some of the iron pellets to slow the bathyscaphe's descent to half a foot a second. It was important to make an easy, smooth landing.

Don Walsh kept his eyes on the depth-finding instruments. Jacques Piccard was posted at one of the tiny windows of the gondola trying to find the sea floor with the beam of the bathyscaphe's searchlight. When the gauge showed 37,500 feet, the depth finder indicated that the *Trieste* was nearing the bottom. Soon afterward, Jacques Piccard said he could see it.

Lieutenant Walsh recorded the depth of the Marianas Trench at 37,800 feet. Later, a careful check of the bathyscaphe's instruments by Navy scientists showed that local conditions in the trench had caused the depth gauges to err by about 2000 feet. The revised official reports of the descent credited Don Walsh and Jacques Piccard with a dive of 35,800 feet.

The sea floor was soft mud. As soon as the *Trieste* landed, the mud rose in a great cloud around the bathyscaphe. For a short time there was total blackness outside. As the cloud was dissipating, Jacques Piccard spied a small red shrimp, about one inch long, floating by.

A few moments later, Don Walsh switched on a light to view the sea bottom through a porthole facing the stern of the bathyscaphe. Only then did he learn what had caused the earthquake-like rocking of the *Trieste*. A window in the tube leading to the conning tower had cracked.

The cracked window presented no immediate danger. During a dive the tube is filled with water, and it makes no difference whether or not the window is watertight. But the men were worried that the shattered window might make it impossible to blow the water out of the tube at the end of the dive. And to leave the bathyscaphe the men would have to climb through this tube into the conning tower. If the tube could not be cleared of water, the men would be imprisoned in the passenger chamber. They thought that they might have to remain there until the *Trieste* had been towed hundreds of miles to Guam where the bathyscaphe could be hoisted out of the sea. Even though the Trieste has a snorkling device so that once on the surface an air supply can be obtained, the hydronauts had no way of knowing how long they would have to stay in the cramped, damp-cold gondola. Their only food was chocolate bars.

They had planned to remain on the bottom for 30 minutes, but soon after discovering the shattered window they started to ascend. They went up fast—4 feet per second. At the bottom, the outside temperature was recorded at 38 degrees. Inside the gondola it was 45 degrees. Mud that had stuck to the bottom of the gondola flew by in an eddy as the *Trieste* went up. Flecks of paint were mixed with the mud. The great pressure at the bottom had compressed the sphere and some of the paint had cracked off. The upward moving cloud of mud and paint gave the men the eerie illusion that the *Trieste* was going down instead of up.

But in a little less than four hours—just before 5 P.M.—the Trieste reached the surface. Slowly and carefully, so as not to jar the window, Lieutenant Walsh worked to empty the water from the exit tube. It seemed a long time before the water level started down. But at last the tube was emptied and the men climbed up the ladder and into the open air.

The successful dive was a carefully planned trial of man's ability to explore the deepest parts of the seas. A submarine can travel thousands of miles under water, but it cannot dive as deep as a bathyscaphe. Thus undersea exploration requires both bathyscaphes and submarines.

Jacques Piccard, at right, and an assistant load iron pellets aboard the *Trieste*.

Chapter 6

Exploration by Submarine

In 1870 Jules Verne, the famous French writer of science fiction, published a book about a submarine. She was named *Nautilus,* and the story of her exploits was entitled *20,000 Leagues Under the Sea.*

Verne's fictional *Nautilus* is a wonderful boat. She has windows through which the undersea's coral gardens, mountains, and sunken ships can be viewed. The commander of the submarine, Captain Nemo, can emerge from his boat whenever he wishes, and hunt in the submerged forests. Sunken treasure ships provide the captain with funds for his expeditions, and fuel is readily obtainable from an extinct volcano on the sea bottom. Toward the end of the book, *Nautilus* reaches the South Pole and while traveling under the ice is trapped by a giant iceberg. Verne gives a thrilling ac-

The modern *Nautilus* was the first submarine to complete an under-ice crossing of the North Pole.

count of how the crew dug the submarine out of the trap. For years readers of *20,000 Leagues Under the Sea* thought the story pure fantasy and did not believe that any real boat could ever penetrate under the polar ice.

Yet in August 1958—less than a century after Jules Verne wrote his story—a real submarine completed a voyage under the North Pole. Like Verne's fictional vessel, the modern boat was named *Nautilus*. Prior to its historic under-ice voyage, the nuclear-powered *Nautilus* had cruised *more* than 20,000 leagues under the sea. (A league equals three nautical miles.)

Verne did much of the research for his book at the French national library, the Bibliothèque Nationale, where he read everything available on submarines, diving gear, and undersea life. Sometimes Verne must have thought there was just too much information to study. The reports about submarines covered a period of centuries. Many men, including the artist-inventor Leonardo da Vinci, had developed plans for underwater boats. Da Vinci kept his submarine drawings a secret, saying he was afraid men would use such a boat for evil purposes.

A boat that can hide under water while attacking

surface shipping is obviously a valuable instrument of war. But from the first there were men who dreamed of peacetime uses. Rev. John Wilkins, an English clergyman, devoted an entire chapter to submarines in a book he published in 1648. He pointed out that a submarine was "serviceable for remote voyages and the carrying of any considerable number of men with provisions and commodities." In 1931, Sir Hubert Wilkins, a direct descendant of the clergyman, made the first actual attempt to navigate a submarine under the North Pole. At that time undersea boats had not yet been sufficiently developed to make such a voyage possible.

A conventional submarine, which operates on battery power when under water, must surface frequently to recharge its batteries. A nuclear-powered submarine can cruise submerged for many days and travel faster than any old-style submarine.

Sir Hubert made his stab under the Arctic ice in a submarine built for duty in World War I and about to be scrapped by the United States Navy. Practically nothing was then known about the Arctic Ocean. Sir Hubert had traveled on top of it by dogsled, and he had also flown over it. But no one had seen the underside of the ice floes. It was assumed they were flat or nearly flat.

During the preparations for the voyage, four parallel runners, similar to sled runners, were attached to the top of the submarine. The runners were supposed to enable the submarine to slide along under the ice. The submarine was also equipped with an ice borer and an exit tube. Sir Hubert planned to drill holes through the ice and climb out to send up balloons for obtaining weather information and to make other scientific studies. The submarine's torpedo room was converted into a laboratory with a hatch through which, theoretically, men wearing diving outfits could step out and walk on the bottom, just as Verne's submariners had done.

This hatch proved very useful to the scientists who made the voyage. Although they did not venture outside into the cold sea, they could, while comfortably seated within the submarine, lower thermometers and other instruments into the water and also draw up samples of it. No one ever before had had such an opportunity to collect data about the ice-covered Arctic Ocean. Although, after traveling only a short distance under the ice, Sir Hubert was forced by mechanical difficulties to turn back, his expedition pointed the way to the making of submarine surveys of the Arctic.

While Commander William R. Anderson, captain of the nuclear-powered submarine *Nautilus,* was cruising under the ice he thought frequently of Sir Hubert and his shipmates. Bill Anderson was glad they had turned back in time. It was obvious to him that the earlier craft and her crude equipment could not have survived a long voyage under the ice.

The electronic equipment on the nuclear-powered *Nautilus* made her a real scientific explorer. She had echo-sounding instruments with twin pens, one to record the profile of the sea bottom and the other the underside of the ice. From some of the ice floes daggers projected downward more than 125 feet. Against such jagged ice, the sled runners that had been fastened to Sir Hubert's submarine would have been completely useless.

The possibility of collision with ice daggers—or with ridges formed when ice floes collide—is an ever-present hazard of under-ice exploration. However, the nuclear-powered *Nautilus* had a sonar eye on her bow that probed ahead through the grey sea and warned of obstacles ahead.

Nautilus had a closed-circuit television set, with the transmitter mounted topside and facing upward. Merely

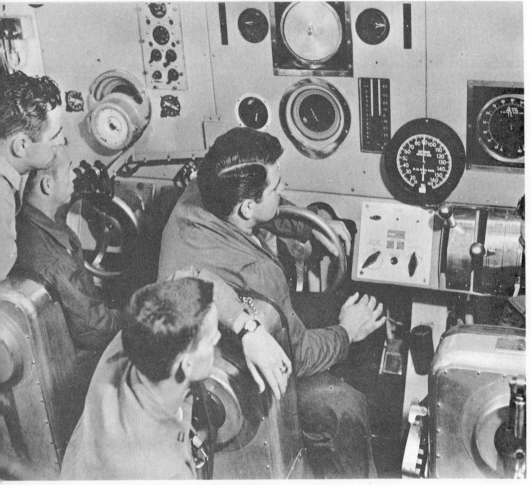

As *Nautilus* explored beneath the Arctic ice, crew members checked their navigational instruments.

by watching the television screen within the submarine, the men could view the underside of the ice floes. When the television camera showed water above—perhaps a little lake encircled by ice—it was safe for the submarine to surface.

Until *Nautilus* went under the ice, comparatively little was known about the depths of the Arctic Ocean, a body of water five times the size of the Mediterranean. Is the bottom of the Arctic Ocean flat or mountainous? The depth-finding instruments aboard *Nautilus* supplied the answers. At the North Pole the sea is 13,410 feet deep. This was about the average depth along the greater part of *Nautilus'* route.

She ran into dangerously shallow water, however, shortly after beginning her under-ice voyage. In one place there was only 45 feet of water below her keel, and less than 25 feet of water between her superstructure and the ice above. *Nautilus* is a big boat, 320 feet long and 50 feet high. If still shallower water lay ahead, the submarine might be trapped between the sea bottom and the ice. Fortunately the submariners were able to extricate themselves by steering into deeper water.

Nautilus discovered a submerged mountain range in the Arctic. The pen on the recording depth finder, which had been showing that the bottom was level and the sea about two miles deep, suddenly indicated humps on the sea floor. The mountain peaks rose higher and higher. For 70 miles *Nautilus* traveled above the mountains while the officers watched anxiously as the depth finder charted the rugged scenery. A depth finder portrays the bottom with vertical exaggeration, which makes the underwater terrain appear steeper than it really is.

"I saw incredibly steep cliffs rise thousands of feet above the ocean floor," Commander Anderson wrote.

During a voyage of exploration in the Arctic Ocean, the atomic submarine *Skate* surfaced through the ice.

U.S. Navy

"Several times I ordered speed slackened, then resumed, as a promontory leveled off or descended as rapidly as it had risen. The shape of these undersea mountains appeared phenomenally rugged, and as grotesque as the craters of the moon."

A short distance before crossing under the North Pole, *Nautilus* traveled over another submerged mountain range called Lomonosov Ridge. It is named for the Russian scientist who predicted its existence from studies of the earth's crust.

Nautilus charted these mountain ranges. The captains of other American submarines which have since made the polar voyage were neither surprised nor startled when they entered the mountainous areas. In fact, the submerged mountains of the Arctic and of other seas are used by submariners to check their positions. Just as captains of surface ships use landmarks for navigational purposes, so men voyaging under the sea pinpoint their position by charted features of the bottom.

Shortly after *Nautilus* was launched, she made a high-speed test run from Key West, Florida, to New London, Connecticut. Because the voyage was made through a part of the Atlantic where the bottom is well mapped, the submarine's navigator was able to check his position with amazing accuracy. The navigator had estimated the time when his boat would pass above a point in the Hudson River undersea canyon. The boat actually arrived there only one minute late.

For detailed charts of the Arctic Ocean, the pioneers who sailed in *Nautilus* supplied more than ten thousand figures on the depth of the water. The chief scientist of the expedition, Dr. Waldo K. Lyon, collected so much information on the temperature of the water, the thickness of the ice, and other important facts that his notes filled two trunks. Every submarine that has dived under the ice since *Nautilus'* first daring voyage has brought back additional information about the Arctic Ocean.

When the nuclear-powered submarine *Triton* circumnavigated the globe in 1960, her captain made many discoveries about the southern oceans. *Triton* followed much the same route sailed by Ferdinand Magellan, commander of the Spanish expedition that completed the first successful round-the-world voyage in 1522. The voyage on the surface route lasted more than three years; the American submarine covered the distance in two months.

Men aboard *Triton* made discoveries completely hidden from Magellan. In the South Atlantic, near Cape Horn at the tip of South America, the submariners cruised over lofty submerged mountains. They found more undersea mountains shortly after the submarine had rounded the cape and entered the South Pacific Ocean.

After completing the circumnavigation of the globe, *Triton* did not head for port. The submarine, without surfacing, continued to cruise for another 10,000 miles. *Triton* remained under water for a total of 84 days.

New submarines are being developed for undersea research. Captain Cousteau's two-man "diving saucer" (left) rests on the deck of his research ship *Calypso*. The Martine submarine (right) is designed for exploration of the ocean floor.

Wide World   UPI

Chapter 7

Treasure Hunters on the Bottom

The colossal figure of Zeus which stands in the lobby of United Nations headquarters in New York City is a replica of an ancient statue found at the bottom of the Aegean Sea. By a lucky coincidence, a diver who had gone down to gather sponges stumbled upon a fragment of the statue. When he brought it to the surface, it was identified as an arm. Later, the massive sculpture was located and raised from its underwater grave. It probably had lain buried there for about 2500 years. Experts say the statue dates from early in the fifth century B.C.

Near the resting place of mighty Zeus, divers found another bronze figure. This one, of a boy jockey, was in nearly perfect condition. However, there were only a few scattered pieces of the horse on which the jockey had been perched. Probably this part of the statue had been shattered when the ship carrying the sculpture from Greece was wrecked near rocky Cape Artemisium.

In ancient times, victorious nations took anything they desired from defeated countries. After Rome conquered Greece, many of the most beautiful Greek statues were loaded on ships for transportation to Rome. Not only the ship carrying the statues of Zeus and the jockey but many others loaded with art treasures, as well as with less precious cargo, foundered on the rocky coasts of the Aegean and Mediterranean seas.

Along all the major shipping routes of bygone days there are wrecks containing treasures of great value. Between 1520 and 1820, when Spanish ships were transporting gold, silver, and other loot from the Americas, Spain's fleets of treasure ships regularly sailed along the treacherous east coast of Florida on their homeward voyage. Some ships were wrecked on the coral reefs and others were sunk by pirates. Only the biggest disasters were recorded. For example, the loss of eight ships of the "flota" commanded by Don Rodrigo de Torres in 1733 was listed in Spanish records and the position of the wrecks was charted. More than two hundred years later a sportsman diver located the remains of three

A diver explores the remains of a ship wrecked off the Florida coast.

of the wrecks. In addition to the Spanish coins called "pieces of eight," he found silver figurines, muskets, crockery, and even parts of the ships' rigging.

Formerly, only professional helmet divers engaged in underwater treasure hunting, and they specialized in salvaging gold and silver. A team of such specialists unloaded the cargo of gold from the steamer *Egypt* which sank in 1921 in the Bay of Biscay. The wreck was 426 feet down, deeper than any diver had ever worked before. But the cargo was valued at $6,000,000, and men were willing to risk their lives to reach the gold bars. Some of the most famous divers of the time were killed during the salvage operation.

Another gold ship, the *Niagara,* sank in 1940 near the New Zealand coast with gold valued at $12,000,000. She lay in even deeper water than the *Egypt.* However, because salvage equipment and techniques had been improved, lifting the gold from the *Niagara* was in some respects easier than salvaging the *Egypt's* cargo. But a live mine caused dangerous complications. The *Niagara* had sunk after hitting a German mine, and another was close to the wreck. The mine was spotted by the diver who had been lowered in an observation chamber to look over the wreck and map the way of getting into the ship's strong room.

The first job was to pull the live mine away from the *Niagara* and blow it up. A helmet diver went down to attach a tow rope to the mine. While he was doing this, his air pipe and life line caught on the horns of the mine. Diver and mine came up directly under the salvage ship and bumped along its keel. The diver knew that at any moment the mine might explode, but he remained calm while trying to disentangle himself. Somehow he got loose, and the mine bobbed up just clear of the salvage ship. It was towed away to a safe distance and then machine-gunned.

Like the majority of sunken ships, the *Niagara* was leaning over on one side. The *Niagara* was lying at such a sharp angle that a hole had to be blasted in her side before divers could enter the room where the gold was stored. The dynamiting had to be done with the greatest of care so that the explosion would not scatter the gold bars. Once the dynamiting was completed, the gold was removed in record time. The unloading, which was done with steel-jawed "grabs," took only seven weeks. It had taken seven years to find the *Egypt* and to remove the gold from the wreck.

Honor Frost, an archaeological draftsman, studies a 1200-year-old ship on the floor of the Mediterranean.

Since the invention of Scuba apparatus, more under-sea treasure hunting is being done than ever before. But when amateur divers search the bottom they are not usually looking for a fortune in gold. The treasures they seek are in a different category. Their objective is the same as that of the experts who dig into Egyptian tombs or into the ruins of ancient cities to find relics of the past. Divers engaged in this fascinating type of de-tective work have brought up from the sea bottom not only masterpieces of art and the personal possessions of sailors and passengers who went down with the ship, but also much valuable information about ancient boats and navigational equipment.

The oldest wreck thus far discovered is believed to date from the late Bronze Age. Experts say the ship sank about 33 centuries ago. The wreck occurred near Bodrum, a Turkish port which in ancient times was called Halicarnassus. Modern Bodrum is the headquar-ters of Turkish sponge divers, and it was one of these men who discovered the Bronze Age ship. He collected pieces of metal from the ship's cargo and tried to sell them as junk. However, as a result of long immersion, the metal was heavily corroded—"rotten," the junk men termed it—and they offered such a low price that the sponge diver did not think it worthwhile to go down for more.

He told this story to Peter Throckmorton, an American photographer-diver who was searching the area for the sites of ancient wrecks. Throckmorton did some scientific detective work and came to the conclusion that the metal pieces which had seemed nearly worthless to the junk dealers were priceless relics. In 1959 Throckmorton explored the wreck with a party of experts, including the director of the Turkish Museum of Archeology at Izmir. They found dozens of ingots—flat rectangular pieces of metal which at one time were used as money. They also found bronze axes, spear points, and sword blades. They even picked up bits of rope made of grass or reed which may have been fastened to the sail when the ship sank.

On subsequent expeditions, Throckmorton hopes that enough will be learned so that a model of the ancient cargo vessel can be constructed. This wreck may supply facts, never known before, about ships that sailed the Mediterranean more than three thousand years ago, hundreds of years before the time when the Greek poet Homer wrote the *Odyssey*.

E. A. Link and his wife Marion are treasure hunters

who spend many months each year searching the sea bottom near the Florida coast and in adjacent areas for old ships and their equipment. In 1955 they made a search for the wreck of Christopher Columbus' flagship. The *Santa Maria* sank, it is believed, near Cape Haitien on the easterly coast of Santo Domingo island. Although the Links found no trace of the *Santa Maria*, they did find an iron anchor from a ship that sailed soon after Columbus' first voyage to America. The date of the iron anchor was established by the United States Bureau of Standards, which analyzed the metal and found that it had been manufactured in the sixteenth century.

Some things rot and disintegrate rapidly after they sink to the bottom, but others can survive thousands of years under the sea. Iron lasts for a long time, but ordinarily wood is preserved only if it is covered by mud or sand.

Many marble statues raised from the sea are pockmarked with holes drilled by the small creatures that crawl on the sea floor. Only the parts of the statues that sink into the mud are shielded.

Many of the iron cannons and cannon balls found in Florida waters are encrusted with coral, but the metal is in good condition. However, after a cannon is hoisted to the surface, it must be quickly treated to prevent disintegration. Because iron is so little affected by submersion, cannons are among the most dependable markers of wrecks. In former days, merchant ships as well as warships were armed with cannons.

Divers are so accustomed to looking for cannons that one man who saw rows of marble pillars on the bottom mistook them for ancient artillery. This led to a particularly rich find near the north coast of Africa. The year was 1913. Apparently a huge Roman ship carrying parts of a Greek temple had been driven off course by stormy weather and had sunk near Tunisia. Its wreckage contained not only the marble columns, but also stone carvings, marble basins, garden vases as high as a man, and many bronze figures. Divers worked five years sending up works of art which are now exhibited in five rooms of the Alaoui Museum at Bardo, Tunisia. When the first expedition was brought to a halt because of lack of funds, many of the heaviest pieces of art were left under water.

Thirty-five years later Captain Cousteau and his French naval team of Scuba divers searched for the wreck again. Although Captain Cousteau had sketches showing where it was supposed to be, he and his expert divers hunted six days before the wreck was found. They knew it was under 127 feet of water, and the search ship cruised around until its echo-sounding instrument showed an area of about that depth. Then divers wearing air tanks, face masks, and foot fins went down to scout along the bottom.

Marcel Ichac

Cousteau's team raised a piece of marble that a Greek sculptor had chiseled over 2000 years earlier.

In order to speed up the search, one man was towed around the entire area on an undersea sled. On the sixth day, Commandant Tailliez was towed on a "shot line," a weighted rope ordinarily used by divers for descending and ascending. As he was pulled under water, he spied a single cylindrical object, tugged his signal rope to indicate "Stop!" and marked the location of the cylinder with a little plastic orange-colored buoy.

According to the records, the first divers who had worked on the wreck had been preparing one column for hoisting and had pulled it away from the others. It was left in this position when the salvage operation was halted. This was the column Commandant Tailliez had marked. The following morning, Captain Cousteau went down and easily located the main wreck.

At the bottom, the marble sculpture looked dark blue and some of the pieces were thickly blanketed with marine growth. But after a thorough scrubbing the marble emerged a snowy white.

Captain Cousteau salvaged two lead parts of an anchor, each weighing three-fourths of a ton. The remainder of the anchor, he believes, was made of wood and had rotted. As a result the design of the old Roman anchor is an unsolved puzzle.

A millstone used by the ship's cook to grind grain was also brought up from the Roman argosy. There were many sections of the wreck where Captain Cousteau's party had no time to search and where he believes tools and many small items may be buried. "We were merely scratching at history's door," he says.

Until quite recently the sites of ancient wrecks were located only by chance. Many were discovered by divers who had gone to the bottom to harvest sponges. Now, however, systematic treasure hunting is being done by divers operating on their own and by groups from diving clubs. News about the location of a wreck is not kept secret but is usually marked on a map. Few of the mapped wreck sites have been completely searched.

Finding a wreck is merely the first step in a salvage operation. Sometimes the discoverer may be lucky enough to see coins or other objects scattered on the sea floor. But ordinarily the wreck and its cargo are hidden under a mound of sand and mud. Digging into a wreck poses many problems, and a salvage boat with special equipment is required.

A diver cannot work with a shovel or pickax. The usual method for removing mud is to wash it away with

An archaeological diver frees an ancient oil container from a ship wrecked about 2000 years ago.

a stream of water pumped down under high pressure. When the bottom is sand, an air hose connected to a compressor on the salvage boat may be used. A diver aims the hose at the area to be cleared.

When small objects are uncovered, they are put into bags or baskets which treasure hunters carry with them. Sometimes the large jugs called amphorae, in which wine and oil were carried in ancient times, are filled with compressed air from the diver's Scuba tank. The jug then bobs to the surface like a balloon. However, large, heavy objects must be hoisted by a derrick. The diver ties a rope around the object and it is then pulled up by men on the salvage boat.

Experienced treasure hunters acknowledge there is nothing easy about undersea archeology. They return from many trips empty-handed. Yet there is always the chance that the next time they may find the equal of the statue of mighty Zeus.

Photographer with pressurized
camera 150 feet below the surface
of the Mediterranean.

Chapter **8**

Underwater Photography

Louis Boutan was one of the most popular faculty
members of the University of Paris summer school.
During the 1893 session, students found the professor's
lectures on biology especially exciting because he frequently mentioned his experiments with underwater
photography.

"Just think how valuable it would be if we were able
to take pictures of fish swimming around and of plants
growing on the bottom," he would say. "Studying dry,
dead specimens does not tell us half of what we should
know. We need pictures of fish and plants in their
natural environment to open our eyes to the true scientific facts."

Professor Boutan was a good underwater swimmer;

95

Auguste Boutan

Louis Boutan took this pioneering photograph of a helmet diver in 1898.

he had learned the technique years before from pearl divers in the South Pacific. The summer school was in Banyuls-sur-Mer, on the north coast of France; its location could not have been more convenient for the professor's photographic experiments. Almost every day, after school hours, the teacher would go for a swim and usually he would return with plants and shells he had plucked from the bottom.

He built a watertight copper box for his camera and in 1893 shot the first underwater pictures ever made. The results were interesting but not good enough to satisfy the photographer. During the following winter he designed a camera that did not need a watertight case. The camera was constructed so that water could circulate through the mechanism. The professor tested this camera in 1894. But Boutan decided he could succeed in making underwater pictures more quickly by using a standard type of camera in a watertight housing. He was pleased with his third photographic outfit. The pictures turned out sharp and clear.

Boutan's undersea photographs created such a sensation that for a while the professor was kept busy explaining his methods and giving interviews to newspaper reporters. To his friends he confided his ambition to take pictures at depths where there is no natural light, where it is always inky black. Even today with modern flash bulbs and electronic lights, illuminating an underwater scene is not easy. Louis Boutan had to start by inventing and constructing submersible lighting equipment.

First he tried lamps which he described as consisting of "a spiral wire of magnesium in a glass balloon containing oxygen and a fine platinum wire, connected to the two poles of the battery." When the current was turned on, the platinum wire became red hot and ignited the magnesium wire, thus producing a brilliant light. (This is the principle of modern flash bulbs.) Professor Boutan decided his flash bulbs were unsatisfactory because they often broke or failed to burn evenly.

The equipment with which he succeeded in lighting an underwater scene consisted of two arc lamps shielded by pressurized housings and activated by storage batteries. The lamps were placed on either side of the camera, which was fastened in a metal framework. Bars extending in front of the camera held a signboard on which the words, "Photographie Sous-Marine à 50 metres"—photography under the sea at 165 feet—had been written. The camera was focused on the sign. After the apparatus had been lowered to a depth of 165 feet, the film was exposed by turning on the arc lights for 10 seconds.

It took an hour to haul up the equipment. While the professor waited, he probably worried about the many things that might have gone wrong. Had the camera been crushed by pressure? And had the lamps produced enough light? They had been tested to operate at twice the depth where the exposure was made, but with remote control one can never be certain whether anything has worked.

"One lamp is full of water," the professor's assistant reported. Fortunately the damage had occurred after the film was exposed, for the picture was evenly lighted and in perfect focus.

The photograph of the sign was displayed at the Paris Exposition in 1900. Although some people regretted that the subject was not more interesting, most people marveled that anyone had succeeded in making an undersea photograph.

Underwater photography became popular after John E. Williamson went below the water line in 1913 to photograph the scenery. Williamson was working as a cartoonist for a newspaper published in Norfolk, Virginia, when his father completed the construction of a telescoping steel tube with an observation sphere at the end. The tube was fitted into the bottom of a barge, and the observation sphere was reached by climbing down through the tube. The equipment was intended for use in salvage operations; a man could sit in the watertight observation sphere and direct divers working outside on sunken ships.

The first time John Williamson climbed down to the sphere, he decided it would make a perfect photographic studio. He looked through one of the windows and saw a fish staring inquiringly at him. The background scenery was seaweed swaying in the current. John persuaded his father that underwater pictures taken from the sphere would be worth more money than might be earned from dozens of salvage operations, and his father obligingly lent the equipment for photographic purposes.

Williamson snapped his first underwater pictures at a depth of 30 feet. He used an ordinary press camera and got such good pictures that he immediately mapped out a plan for making an underwater movie.

He proposed to make a documentary film in which fish would be the principal actors. As soon as a new sphere had been built—he called it a photosphere—Williamson left for the Bahama Islands. He selected this area because of the clarity of its water and the dazzling whiteness of the sea bed. These are the conditions that produce the most beautiful undersea pictures and that have made the Bahamas one of the favorite locales for undersea photography.

The warm, blue-green water in the Bahama area is infested with sharks. Williamson considered this an advantage. He had promised his financial backers a sequence showing a fight between a man and a shark, and it was handy to have some of the big grey brutes prowling around.

In order to lure sharks to his photosphere, Williamson used a dead horse as bait. The sharks slashed into it, and when the bait was pulled away the sharks whirled around in a frenzy. At this moment a native diver, who was waiting for a signal that sharks were within camera range, plunged in. Williamson began to crank his camera as the diver approached a mean-looking shark, swam below it, and circled, poised for the moment when he could thrust his knife into the shark. Suddenly Williamson yelled: the man and the fish had disappeared. The photographer ran to another

An oil geologist, wearing Scuba equipment and a weight belt, photographs the floor of the sea.

Shell Oil

window and saw the diver slit the shark's belly, but he had no time to get his camera into position to take pictures.

When the diver refused to risk his life a second time, Williamson decided that he himself would have to fight a shark. In recounting the experience, the photographer said that as a shark came for him he looked into the camera window and knew that, whatever happened to him, his fight with the shark would be recorded on film. The picture turned out to be a real thriller. It showed Williamson grasping the monster's fin and then thrusting his knife into its white belly.

The first showing of his movie was in 1914 at the Smithsonian Institution in Washington. The audience of top-ranking scientists was enthralled. After the lights had been turned on in the auditorium, there was much talk about the scientific value of Williamson's photosphere.

The scientists realized that the photosphere had, in effect, turned the sea into an aquarium. From the sphere, fish could be observed and photographed as conveniently as if they were swimming in a fish bowl.

For many years scientists made good use of the photosphere. From talking to them, as well as from his own observations, Williamson became an expert on undersea life. He was especially interested in sharks and studied their method of attack. He disproved the theory that, because of the position of their mouths, sharks must roll over before moving in for a kill. Williamson said that sharks can slash off a mouthful while swimming in normal position with the dorsal fin upright.

Williamson's photosphere could be moved slowly under water. As the barge to which the photosphere was attached traveled along the surface, people riding below in the photosphere enjoyed a comfortable sightseeing trip. Usually, however, the barge remained at anchor and the cameramen waited, patiently or otherwise, until fish swam into view.

Professor Boutan's idea of a camera that could be operated by a diver, or suspended in the water, had many advantages. Even though one could sit as comfortably in the photosphere as in a living room, a free diver could swim down with a camera into deeper water. And an automatic camera could be lowered into depths where no diver dared venture. But the mechanical and technical problems involved in designing submersible camera equipment could not be quickly solved.

Waterproofing a camera is only one part of the problem. A number of methods have been developed for keeping a camera dry, the simplest being to insert the camera into a plastic bag. Stores that carry supplies for Scuba divers sell such bags. Also, a homemade enclosure can be devised for use in shallow water. One ingenious boy put his Brownie box camera into a light-colored rubber glove, sealed a plexiglass disk onto it, and shot underwater photographs through the disk.

Such an arrangement is satisfactory if the photographer is operating only a few feet under the surface. But a camera used in deep water must be protected against pressure as well as water. Professor Boutan attached an inflated balloon to his camera; when the air within the camera case was compressed by the weight of the water above it, the air from the balloon was drawn in. The balloon method has been tried by modern photographers and they have also used cylinders of compressed air to equalize the pressure within the camera.

But the usual way of protecting a deep-sea camera from the effects of water pressure is to encase it in a thick-walled tube. The tube may also contain an electronic

Underwood & Underwood
National Academy of Sciences

A camera is lowered from a research vessel (left). Such a camera has photographed valuable manganese 2½ miles down (right).

flash unit. The equipment is fastened to strong metal frames and the camera is angled so that the picture will show a wide area of the bottom.

One picture, taken 2½ miles down in the central Pacific shows pebbles believed to be composed of valuable manganese oxide. Other lucky photographs have disclosed the presence of currents flowing over the bottom. The direction of a strong current is shown by hollows on one side of pebbles.

Cameras used for deep-sea photography are amazing mechanisms; they can roll the film after an exposure has been made, and some can even switch one lens for another. However, since the operation of these cameras is completely mechanical, they photograph whatever happens to be within focus. Even if it has taken an entire day to lower and to retrieve a deep-sea camera, and all parts of the mechanism have worked perfectly, the pictures may show nothing of outstanding interest.

This difficulty may be eliminated by television. When a cameraman can view the underwater scenery on a television screen before taking a picture, he can choose the particular subject or scene he wishes to photograph. Closed-circuit underwater television systems have been successfully used for several years. Ships engaged in scientific research have television cameras fastened to their keels which transmit, by direct wire to a screen within the ship, views of the water and sometimes of the sea bottom. The range of submarine television equipment is still limited, but before long inventors may devise equipment to televise the deepest parts of the oceans.

In undersea exploring, a camera may be a better observer than a diver, for a camera frequently can see what the human eye cannot. For instance, not until the first color pictures were shot at depths of 100 feet and more was it discovered that the deep-sea plants and animals are brightly colored. Some authorities estimate that red light waves penetrate only to about 30 feet below the surface, orange to about 50 feet, violet to about 80 feet, yellow to about 200 feet, and blue to about 250 feet. In deeper water, everything looks bluish-green or black to the human eye.

Living coral looks blue to divers, and for a long time it was believed that coral changed color when brought to the surface. The color films exposed with bright electronic flashes revealed that no such change occurs. Under the sea, coral is as bright and as red as we see it in our own atmosphere. Pictures snapped far below the sea's surface reveal an underwater world of brilliant color.

A Scuba-diving photographer takes undersea movies.

Chapter 9

The Search for Oil Beneath the Sea

The Gulf of Mexico is dotted with man-made islands, some as big as a football field and all topped with high skeleton towers. Many of these islands are perched on stilts about 40 feet above the surface of the sea. When the stilts are pulled up, the island floats on the water and, like an ordinary barge, can be towed from place to place. Several have been towed halfway around the world. These man-made islands are taken wherever an undersea oil well is to be drilled.

There are many types of offshore drilling rigs, but all have the huge skeleton towers required for drilling oil wells on land or under the sea. These towers, because

This mobile oil-drilling rig was towed 6800 miles from Germany to the Persian Gulf.
British Petroleum

of their very height—some are as tall as a 20-story building—can be hazardous at sea. In hurricanes and other storms, the men who live and work on the barges have cause for worry about the effect of the howling winds on the vulnerable skeleton towers.

The lure that leads men to invest millions in offshore oil operations is the vast and yet unmeasured reservoir of petroleum under the continental shelf. Some experts estimate that under the Gulf of Mexico alone there are ten billion barrels of oil; there may be more oil under water than under all the continental land areas of the earth.

All of our world's oil fields were once covered by ancient seas. The oil was formed from plant and animal matter that sank to the sea bottom millions of years ago. As the layers of organic matter built up, they were squeezed and compressed by the weight of the layers above. The heat created by the pressure, together with bacterial and chemical action, turned all the tiny particles into petroleum.

Since oil is always found in marine sediments, geologists guessed there were rich oil deposits under existing oceans. The problem was how to find the undersea oil and, once it was found, how to drill a well. The technique of undersea oil prospecting and of tapping the

In the Gulf of Mexico, an oil-company geophysicist (left) studies a seismic record, and a geologist (right) takes specimens from the bottom.

petroleum was developed in the Gulf of Mexico. The first large-scale underwater drilling operation started there in 1934.

Now undersea oil is being tapped in many parts of the world—in the South China Sea off the coast of Borneo, in the Persian Gulf, in the coastal waters of California, and in the Caspian Sea where Russians are operating. The oil-drilling platforms are moving farther and farther offshore. In the beginning they stayed close to land, but today they are working in deep water, 50 or 60 miles from the coast.

When an oil prospector goes to sea, he uses the same

technique he would apply if he were hunting for oil underground. He starts by making a seismic survey. Since the 1920's, oil prospectors working on land have been mapping underground formations by setting off blasts of dynamite. The resulting shock waves are recorded by the prospector's seismograph. This instrument was invented to record the waves created by natural earthquakes and is still used for that purpose. When prospectors manufacture earthquakes with dynamite, the seismograph indicates the type of rock layers which the shock waves have hit. Geologists know what formations are apt to contain oil, and a seismic survey tells them where to drill.

On land, a series of holes, each about 30 to 150 feet deep, must be dug for the charges of dynamite. When scouting for oil under the sea, prospectors merely drop depth bombs. Like oceanographers mapping the sea bed, the oil prospectors often travel on two boats; the dynamite is dropped from one of the boats and the recording equipment is carried on the other.

An expert crew of oil prospectors can complete a seismic survey of the sea floor more rapidly than a similar study can be made on land. But although the actual surveying is easier, there is one big problem that makes maritime prospecting far more difficult than scouting on land.

On shore there are many landmarks, but at sea all waves look alike. Like other sailors, the men hunting oil under the sea use charts and other navigational aids to locate their position, and they must navigate with absolute accuracy. If a big passenger ship is a tenth of a mile off course, the error is usually not serious. But if the navigator of a small seismic survey boat were to make a similar mistake, the loss to the oil company might mount to millions of dollars. Although there may be an oil field close to where the drilling rig is set up, the oil may not be found.

Both ashore and afloat, oil prospectors chart underlying rock formations with gravimeters, which measure gravity, and with magnetometers, which measure magnetism. Generally, rocks that may contain oil are less magnetic than harder rocks that never contain oil. Gravimeters can detect tiny differences in the weight of rocks. They also indicate where there are salt domes. These, especially in the Gulf of Mexico, are natural markers of petroleum deposits. Salt domes are far lighter in weight than any rock under which they happen to be buried. When the gravimeter indicates a particularly low pull, a prospector may conclude he has located a salt dome.

A gravimeter is lowered to the sea bottom, but a magnetometer is trailed behind the oil prospectors' boat. This detecting device may also be towed by an airplane. An area between Florida and Cuba was rapidly surveyed in this way.

Before starting to drill a well, oil companies frequently want a firsthand inspection of the sea bottom. There are divers who make a specialty of such work. When one sheik granted permission to prospect for oil in

Divers (left) descended to the floor of the Persian Gulf in this shark-proof cage. Two or three miles of piping (right) may be lowered to an undersea oil field.

British Petroleum   Arabian American Oil Company

the Persian Gulf, the oil company hired a team of divers to chip off samples of rocks and to take photographs. The area was infested with sharks and the divers descended in cages. Before a diver stepped out of the cage and went to work, he made sure no man-eaters were cruising in the immediate vicinity. If one did appear, the diver could retreat to his cage.

Because close-up inspection by divers has proved so valuable, oil companies are sending their top-ranking prospectors to diving school. Many of these geologists have become expert divers. These men go down with a bag packed with geologists' hammers, cameras, and sometimes glass jars in which they catch bubbles of natural gas rising from the sea floor. In accordance with the approved system for Scuba diving, prospectors work in two-men teams; a third man, who remains on the boat, keeps track of the divers and hoists up the samples they have collected.

In the United States, when an oil company finds a promising site, it arranges with the owner of the property for permission to drill. But the sea bed off the American coasts is publicly owned. Anyone has the right to explore it, but no one may proceed with the drilling of a well until government authorities announce they are ready to lease the undersea land. Usually these leases are for lots of about 5000 acres and the interested companies submit their bids. The one offering the highest price is awarded the lease. The next step is to bring a drilling rig to the place where the first well is to be dug.

The drill pipe is made up of many sections; each is about 30 feet long and weighs about 300 pounds. A large bit is fastened to the bottom of the pipe. (The bit is like the one in a dentist's drill, though hundreds of times larger and stronger.) The pipe is lowered from the top of the skeleton tower. When the bit reaches the sea floor, an engine starts rotating the pipe. As the bit cuts into the sea bed, the pipe is lengthened by attaching additional sections to it. Sometimes as much as two or three miles of piping is needed to grind into the oil reservoir.

The drill pipe is encased in larger pipes and all are protected by heavy coatings of cement. From the data supplied by the prospectors, the engineers know approximately how deep a hole must be drilled before there is a chance of striking oil. Nevertheless they continuously study the "cuttings" forced up through the pipes to find out what kind of sand, mud, and stone the drill is biting into. In every examination of the grindings, the men look for fossilized particles of the tiny organisms which often are found in or near oil-bearing rock.

Months may be spent in drilling a well. To reach the oil in one well in the Gulf of Mexico, a 10,000-foot hole had to be drilled. It took 74 days to do this; the cost amounted to more than half a million dollars. And until the well was tapped, no one knew whether the work and expense were justified. For—as on land—a well drilled in the sea bed may prove to contain neither oil nor gas.

When a drilling operation is successful, crude oil flows up from the well. But the flow is checked as soon as enough oil has been collected for testing purposes. The oil flow is stopped by turning the cut-off valves in a massive arrangement known as a "Christmas Tree." Before a well is put into production, a transportation system must be arranged for carrying the oil to storage tanks ashore.

Shipping oil from undersea wells in tankers might seem to be the most practical and economical system of transportation. But there is a better way of conveying undersea oil to the mainland. This is by pipe line. A vast network of pipes has been built to carry oil across country, and pipe lines have also been laid in the sea floor.

Although underwater pipe lines are normally laid on

Arabian American Oil Company

An offshore oil worker in the Persian Gulf adjusts the "Christmas tree."

the sea bed, in some instances they must be buried in the mud. Sinking pipes into the bed of the sea is infinitely more complicated than digging a trench in a field and lowering a pipe into it.

At first, trenches for undersea pipe lines were dug with ordinary dredging equipment. After a trench had been dredged, the pipe was lowered into it. The difficulty of lowering the pipe and lining it up correctly in the trench made the operation entirely impractical.

The problem was solved by S. V. Collins, who invented a jet-action apparatus to dig a trench and simultaneously lay the piping in it. The Collins trencher has nozzles through which water and air are forced at high pressure. This jetting action cuts the trench. The piping is attached behind the trencher. As it is pulled over the sea floor by a surface ship, a trench is opened up and the piping is laid in it. Oil pipes are often big —ranging up to 30 inches in diameter—but the Collins trencher can lay more than five miles of underwater piping in a single day.

It is not necessary to lay separate pipes from each oil well to the storage tanks. One pipe-line system can be used to carry the oil produced by many wells. From each new well a section of piping is laid to the main pipe line, which carries all the oil to the tanks on shore.

Chapter 10

Wiring the Oceans

Nowadays, sending a cablegram via an undersea wire has become commonplace. Even submerged telephone wires are taken for granted. Yet the metal cables which carry telegraphic signals and the human voice from continent to continent are, in fact, miracles of oceanic engineering.

Men began to dream about transmitting messages through underwater cables shortly after telegraph wires were strung overland. When Cyrus M. Field began to work on the project in 1854, the easiest part was selecting the route for the cable. Lieutenant Matthew F. Maury, chief of what is now called the United States Hydrographic Office, recommended a route that had been surveyed the summer before. Maury had sent out research ships to make soundings in the Atlantic, and a ridge or plateau had been found on the sea bottom. It extends all the way from Newfoundland to Ireland.

In this area the average depth of the sea is only two miles.

The plateau—which Maury named "Telegraphic Plateau"—is in the northern foothills of the largest of Earth's mountain ranges. Known as the Mid-Atlantic Range, these almost wholly submerged mountains stretch for 10,000 miles in a north-south direction from the Arctic to the Antarctic. The range is twice as wide as the Andes. A few of the highest peaks of the underwater mountains rise above the sea and are shown on maps as oceanic islands. The Azores are crests of the Mid-Atlantic Range, and so also are the craggy islets near the Equator called the Rocks of St. Paul.

Underwater telegraph cables had already been laid in water as deep as that over the plateau, but the length of the transatlantic cable posed problems such as never before had been encountered. To span the Atlantic, 2500 miles of copper cable were needed. Each mile of the cable weighed a ton. Since there was no one ship capable of carrying and of laying 2500 tons of cable, two ships—one English, the other American—were chosen for the job.

On August 4, 1857, the eastern end of the Atlantic cable was made fast at Valentia, Ireland. The next morning the U.S.S. *Niagara,* the largest steam frigate in the world, started for Newfoundland, slowly reeling out the cable as it steamed westward. The *Niagara* had covered only five miles when the cable caught in the deck machinery and broke. The ship turned back, made another start, and for 335 miles all went well. Then, while trying to check the speed with which the cable was sliding into the sea, the brake was applied too rapidly, and the cable broke. That ended the attempt to lay a cable in 1857.

Months before, Cyrus Field had been asked what he would do if the wire were to break and be lost in the sea. He replied: "Charge it to profit and loss and go to work to make another."

He did exactly that. While more wire was being manufactured, the experts made many improvements in the cable-laying machinery. The following spring, before tackling the Atlantic again, the cable ships sailed for the Bay of Biscay where they practiced reeling out wire and retrieving broken pieces. (This same practice area was used in 1955, before telephone wires were pulled across the Atlantic.)

In June 1858, the cable fleet again assembled at

Valentia, Ireland, and this time succeeded in laying a cable across the Atlantic. One end of the cable was hooked up to the receiving and transmitting station at Valentia. The western end of the wire was connected with the telegraph house in the Bay of Bulls, Newfoundland, 1950 miles away.

There was great excitement when the news was announced. But although the public was thrilled the experts were worried; they knew something was wrong with the cable. The signals came through so garbled that they were difficult to decipher. Even worse, for hours at a time no messages came through at all. Twenty-seven days after the cable had been hooked up, it failed completely and finally. The dead cable still lies on the bottom of the Atlantic.

Some of the experts believed that too high an electrical charge had been used to send the cable messages and that a part of the wire had been burned out. Others maintained the wire had broken a few hundred miles from Ireland, where the continental shelf ends and there is a precipitous drop in the sea bottom. The arguments continued for years, but at no time did anyone attempt to fish up a piece of the wire to try to find

The *Great Eastern* laid the first successful telegraph cable across the Atlantic.

out just what had gone wrong. Such a fishing expedition would have been both difficult and costly, and millions had already been spent on the cable.

Yet Cyrus Field continued to believe that a trans-ocean cable not only was possible but also would be profitable. In July 1865, he was ready for the third try at wiring the Atlantic. The *Great Eastern*, five times larger than any steamer built up to that time (she was designed to carry 4000 passengers), was the cable ship.

The 1865 cable was far better constructed than either the first or the second one. The conductor core and the insulation were heavier, and particular care had been taken with the outer protective sheathing. But there were a few imperfections in the wire. When the *Great Eastern* had laid more than two-thirds of the cable and was only 600 miles from Newfoundland, a faulty length of wire slipped through. In the attempt to

Aboard a modern cable ship, Peruvian seamen work with two kinds of grapples.

American Cable & Radio

pull it back, the cable broke. This time the chief cable
engineer tried to retrieve the broken wire. To do so he
would have to hook the cable, hidden from sight, miles
under water. Even today, with modern equipment,
fishing up a broken cable is a colossal task.

The grappling hook lowered from the *Great Eastern*
was fastened to five miles of wire rope. It took two
hours for the iron grapple to reach the bottom. Then
the *Great Eastern* sailed back and forth over the place
where the cable was thought to lie. The search started
at five o'clock in the evening and continued throughout
the night. Early in the morning the grapple hooked
into the cable, but after it had been raised about a mile
from the bottom, the strain was too great for the grappling equipment. When it broke, the cable, the grapple,
and several miles of the wire "fishing line" dropped to
the bottom. The same thing happened several days
later when another grapple hooked the cable. The loss
of the second grapple left the *Great Eastern* without the
necessary equipment to continue the search. After put-
ting out two buoys as markers, the ship headed back for
England.

Field, who had now failed three times, still would

not admit defeat. His plan for the following year was to lay a new cable and to complete the one that had broken. On July 13, 1866, the *Great Eastern* again sailed westward from Valentia Bay, spooling out the new cable. Fourteen days later she arrived in the Newfoundland harbor appropriately named Heart's Content, having at last placed a successful cable across Telegraph Plateau.

There was one job still to be completed. The *Great Eastern* went back to sea to grapple for the cable that had broken the year before. She had the best equipment available for the search, including 20 miles of wire rope capable of standing a 30-ton strain. For days there was no sign of the lost cable. The grapple was lowered thirty times before it hooked the cable. It was hoisted aboard and a new length of cable was spliced on to the old. Then the *Great Eastern* sailed for Newfoundland and completed the laying of the second Atlantic cable.

When the broken cable was lifted to the deck of the *Great Eastern,* the part of the wire that had sunk into the ooze on the sea floor was a muddy white. The rest was the original black. This was a good omen, for it indicated the ocean bed was firm enough so that some of the cable would remain on the top of the sea floor from which it could be fished up if repairs became necessary.

The first cables required no servicing for five years, and the record since then has been even better. There is a section of cable in mid-Atlantic, put down in 1873, on which no repair has yet been made. But in 1929 most of the transatlantic cables broke. An underwater avalanche is thought to have caused a turbidity current —a stream of mud, sand, and rocks—which destroyed everything in its path.

There is no way to protect cables from deep-sea up-heavals nor from damage by animal life. There have been fourteen known instances when sperm whales have broken cables. One of these breaks occurred where the cable was under three miles of water. When the repair ship raised the cable, a 45-foot whale was entangled in it. Scientists suggested that the whale may have mis-taken the coils of the cable for the tentacles of a giant squid which whales hunt on the bottom. From a scien-tific point of view the entire affair was interesting be-cause it had not previously been known that whales, which are air-breathing mammals, could dive to such great depths. However, for the cable company, the record dive of the sperm whale merely meant an expensive repair job.

As long as telephone conversations across the Atlantic were transmitted by short-wave radio, reception was both noisy and undependable. Then, in 1956, the first transocean telephone cable was completed. It became possible to talk to someone in Europe as easily as we do to someone around the corner.

By the time plans were made to lay the telephone wires between America and Europe, there were so many cables crisscrossing the bottom of the Atlantic that choosing the new routes posed quite a problem. A telegraph cable can carry messages in two directions at the same time, but a deep-sea telephone wire is a one-way line. It can carry many messages simultaneously, but they must all go in the same direction. If you are in the United States and receive a telephone call from a friend in London, your voice will be carried by one wire. His voice will travel through a twin wire located twenty or thirty miles away on the bed of the sea.

In the Atlantic telephone cables, there are bulges every 40 miles containing complicated instruments. Each one amplifies the voice currents passing through it about a million times. Transmitting the human voice

At the Newfoundland end, the first transatlantic telephone cable was pulled ashore from the British ship *Monarch*.

Men load miles of cable aboard a cable ship.

under the sea became possible only after these electronic devices were perfected.

On long-distance overland wires, the voice is also boosted at regular intervals, but building amplifiers for undersea service involves many special problems. The amplifiers must withstand three tons of pressure per square inch when they lie on the sea bottom; yet they must be as flexible as the cable into which they are spliced, so that the cable can be unreeled without stops or interruptions. It is expected that the amplifiers in the Atlantic telephone lines will require no servicing for at least twenty years.

Built into the amplifiers is a special circuit used for testing purposes. These circuits not only indicate that each individual amplifier is performing at maximum efficiency, but also give information about the water temperature. Thus, for scientific purposes, the telephone amplifiers are as valuable as if a string of thermometers were stretched along the sea bed.

The cables in the Pacific lie in deeper water than do those in the Atlantic Ocean; in some places they are under 3½ miles of water. The deeper the water, the more difficult it is to put down a cable. However, in choosing a cable route, depth of water is only one of many considerations. Most important is avoiding areas with steep precipices and submarine canyons. Now, before selecting a cable route, survey ships equipped with depth finders are sent out to map the bottom. The charts they make show where the cable should be detoured to avoid submerged mountains or the best place to cross a canyon.

In addition to depth finders, deep-sea cameras and many other instruments developed for oceanographic research are being used by the cable companies. And they in turn, while solving the practical problems of wiring the oceans, are contributing greatly to our knowledge of the undersea world.

Two deep-sea explorers wait to be picked up after a record-breaking descent in the bathyscaphe *Trieste*.

Chapter 11

Earth's Last Frontier

These are pioneering days in the exploration of the world beneath the sea. Great discoveries are being made in rapid succession.

A submarine cruising under the ice-covered Arctic Ocean finds a lofty range of submerged mountains. Shortly afterward, a depth recorder on a surface ship

U.S. Navy

discloses a sunken island in the Atlantic near the west coast of Africa. Scientists estimate that the island sank about 10,000 years ago, at the end of Earth's last glacial period. When the ice melted, the sea level of the Atlantic rose about 250 feet and the island was covered by water.

At one time it was thought that no living creatures lived in the deepest part of the sea. Now, however, we have proof that animals of many kinds live at great depths. Many of the fish brought up from the bottom are oddities. One, for instance, was shaped like a teardrop, measured two inches in length, and had large blue eyes. Other inhabitants of the deeps resemble fish commonly found in shallower water. Scientists guess that at some time members of certain fish families moved down into the cold, lightless realms of the ocean and became adapted to conditions there. But what is the reason for the migration?

Such mysteries of the sea will be solved when scientists piece together the story of the oceans from the many clues they are gathering. The answers will do far more than merely satisfy human curiosity. Many facts discovered about the undersea world have a practical value.

For example, it is known that some of the fish that make up our food supply feed on the tiny organisms called plankton. The fish congregate wherever plankton is most abundant. By tracking the movement of plankton, scientists can advise commercial fishermen where to set their nets.

Sea water contains small quantities of gold, though no practical method has yet been developed for extracting the precious metal. However, the seas' other minerals and chemicals may prove of far greater importance than its gold. Underwater oil and gas wells have already been tapped, and the search for other valuable resources is under way.

Near his shark-proof cage in the Persian Gulf, an oil geologist chips samples from the bottom.

British Petroleum

Many kinds of exploration are dangerous, but the explorers who go down into the sea face special perils. Divers, submariners, and the men who ride to the bottom in bathyscaphes depend on the correct functioning of many mechanical devices. These sea explorers, like the astronauts preparing to soar into outer space, must be ready to risk their lives.

Seagoing scientists haul in a plankton net to obtain information about the life of the sea.

U.S. Navy

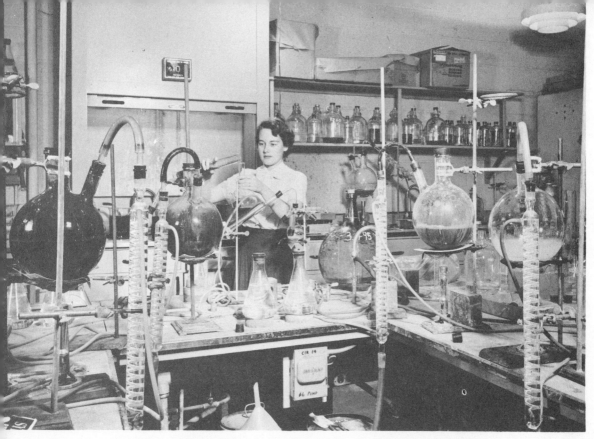

National Academy of Sciences

Oceanographic research is continued in a laboratory ashore, as samples of sea water are chemically analyzed.

Of course, not everyone who devotes himself to the science of the sea goes down to the bottom or even makes an exploratory voyage in a surface research ship. Many experts in the field of oceanography work in laboratories ashore, where they solve scientific riddles by piecing together bits of evidence taken from the sea.

There is a spirit of cooperation among the scientists of the many nations sponsoring oceanographic research.

When an exploratory expedition is being planned by one country, it is not unusual to invite experts from other countries to join the expeditionary party. Thus an American scientist may travel on a Danish research ship, or a Swedish expert on a French ship.

To aid the exchange of information, scientists organized the International Oceanographic Congress. Its first session was held in 1959 at the United Nations headquarters in New York City. Russian scientists came to New York on one of their country's newest research ships. France sent one of her famous scientific research vessels to New York. At nearby piers were two American oceanographic ships. All the ships were open for inspection by the scientists attending the International Oceanographic Congress. The visitors were shown the equipment used for probing the sea. They exchanged opinions on techniques and methods.

The ships remained in New York harbor only a short time. There is so much exploring to do that a research vessel must be kept at work. Scientists are eagerly pushing into new territory. They know that today we are just beginning the exploration of the undersea world.

Suggestions for Further Reading

RACHEL CARSON. *The Sea Around Us,* edited by Anne Terry White. Golden Press.

JAMES FISHER. *The Wonderful World of the Sea.* Garden City Books.

FERDINAND C. LANE. *All About the Sea.* Random House.

JACQUES YVES COUSTEAU. *The Silent World.* Harper & Brothers.

JAMES DUGAN. *Man Under the Sea.* Harper & Brothers.

PIERRE DE LATIL AND JEAN RIVOIRE. *Man and the Underwater World.* G. P. Putnam's Sons.

FRANCIS P. SHEPARD. *The Earth Beneath the Sea.* Johns Hopkins Press.

HELEN RAITT. *Exploring the Deep Pacific.* W. W. Norton & Co.

ANTON J. BRUUN and others. *The Galathea Deep Sea Expedition.* Macmillan Company.

WILLIAM BEEBE. *Half Mile Down* (bathysphere). Duell, Sloan & Pearce.

GEORGES HOUOT AND PIERRE WILLM. *2000 Fathoms Down* (bathyscaphe). E. P. Dutton & Co.

WILBUR CROSS. *Challengers of the Deep* (submarines). William Sloane Associates.

WILLIAM R. ANDERSON WITH CLAY BLAIR, JR. *Nautilus 90 North.* World Publishing Co.

MARION C. LINK. *Sea Diver: A Quest for History Under the Sea.* Rinehart & Co.

JERRY GREENBERG. *Underwater Photography Simplified.* Seahawk Products, P.O. Box 1157, Coral Gables, Florida.

ARTHUR C. CLARKE. *Voice Across the Sea* (cables). Harper & Brothers.

142

About the author of this book

Ruth Brindze was born in New York City, attended its public schools, and is a graduate of the Columbia University School of Journalism. She lives with her husband, a lawyer, in Mt. Vernon, New York. Together they enjoy cruising on their sailboat "Erewhon."

Miss Brindze writes: "Next best to being on and in the sea, I enjoy writing about it. Of the many books I have written, those about the sea and boats are my favorites." Among these books are *Seamanship Below Deck, Boating Is Fun, The Experts' Book of Boating,* and *The Story of the Trade Winds.*